CEO'S FINANCIAL METRICS PLAYBOOK

Keeping Your **Eye** on the **Pulse** of Your Business

GARY TAKACS
CEO UNIVERSITY®

Contents

Acknowledgements 1

Introduction 3

Accounts Payable Turnover Ratio 5
How do you pay your suppliers? 5
Accounts Payable Turnover Ratio explained 5
Accounts Payable Turnover Ratio calculated 6
Accounts Payable Turnover Ratio application 7

Accounts Receivable Turnover Ratio 9
Are your debtors a safe bet? 9
Accounts Receivable Turnover explained 9
Accounts Receivable Turnover calculated 10
Accounts Receivable Turnover interpreted 11

Accounts Payable Turnover Ratio 13
How soon do you pay? 13
Accounts Payable Turnover Ratio explained 13
Accounts Payable Turnover Ratio calculation 14
A common error to avoid 15
Accounts Payable Turnover Ratio application 15

Asset Utilization Ratio 17
Utilizing assets efficiently 17
Asset Utilization Ratio explained 17
Asset Utilization Ratio calculated 18
Asset Utilization Ratio interpreted 18
Asset Utilization Ratio application 19

Bad Debt Ratio 21
Managing your debtors efficiently 21
Bad Debt Ratio explained 22
Bad Debt Ratio calculated 22
Bad Debt-to-Accounts Receivable Ratio 22
Bad Debt-to-Sales Ratio 23
Bad Debt Ratio interpreted 23
Bad Debt Ratio application 24

Cash Flow Ratios 25
Do you know how much accessible cash you need available
    to pay upcoming expenses? 25
Cash Flow Ratios explained 25
Operating Cash Flow Ratio calculation 26

Cash Flow Margin calculation 26
Price-to-Cash Ratio 27
Cash Flow Solvency 27
Cash Flow Return on Assets 27

Current Ratio 31
What is the proportion of current assets to current liabilities? 31
Current Ratio explained 31
Current Ratio calculated 32
Current Ratio interpreted 33

Current Liability Ratio 35
Determine your ability to settle short-term obligations 35
Current Liability Ratio explained 35
Current Liability Ratio calculated 36
Current Liability Ratio interpreted 37
Current Liability Ratio application 37

Days of Inventory Outstanding 39
How good are you at turning inventory into sales? 39
DIO explained 39
DIO calculated 40
The nuances of DIO 41

Days Sales Outstanding 43
How quickly do you collect payments once you make a sale? ... 43
DSO explained 43
DSO calculated 44

DSO application 44
The nuances of DSO 45

Days of Working Capital 47

Convert capital to revenue more quickly 47
Days of Working Capital explained 47
Days of Working Capital calculated 48
Days of Working Capital interpreted 49

Depreciation 51

The act of writing-down assets 51
Depreciation explained 51
Use Case Depreciation Formula 52
Straight-Line Depreciation Formula 52
Declining Balance Depreciation Formula 53
Sum-of-the-Years' Digits Depreciation Formula 54
Usage-Based Depreciation Formula 55
Depreciation application 56

Fixed Asset Ratios 57

Assessing asset performance 57
Fixed Asset Ratios explained 57
Fixed Asset Ratios calculated 58
Fixed Assets to Net Worth Ratio 58
Fixed Assets Turnover Ratio 59
Fixed Asset Ratios application 60

Gross Income Multiplier 61
Assessing rental property 61
Gross Income Multiplier explained 61
GIM calculated 62
Gross Income Multiplier Formula: 62
GIM Formula application 63
GIM Formula limitations 63

Gross Profit Variance 65
A great checkpoint for business performance 65
Gross Profit Variance explained 65
Gross Profit Variance calculated 66
Gross Profit Variance application 68

Growth Ratio 69
Figuring out how much your company can grow 69
Growth Ratio explained 69
Growth Ratio calculated 69
Growth Ratio interpreted 71

Indirect Labor to Direct Labor 73
Assessing labor cost efficiency 73
Direct/Indirect Labor explained 73
Indirect Labor to Direct Labor Ratio calculated 74
Is there a problem? 75
Direct/Indirect Labor Ratio application 75

Inventory Ratios 77
Assessing how your inventory works for you 77
Inventory ratios explained 77
Inventory Turnover Ratio formulas 78
Inventory Turnover calculated 78
Average Inventory calculated 78
Inventory Turnover interpretation 79
Days' Inventory on Hand Ratio 79
Days' Inventory on Hand Ratio calculated 79
Inventory Period calculation 80
Inventory Ratio application 80

Off-Balance-Sheet Assets and Liabilities 83
The impact they have on a business 83
Opening the book on "off-book" 83
Operating leases explained 84
Partnerships explained 84
Their impact on ratios 85
Concept versus application 85

Operating Assets Ratio 87
Understanding the role of productive assets 87
Operating Assets Ratio explained 87
Operating Assets Ratio calculated 87
Operating Assets Ratio application 89

Opportunity Cost 91
Understanding the value of missed opportunities 91

- Opportunity cost explained 91
- Examples of opportunity cost 92
- Opportunity cost application 93

Payback Period 95
- When will I start getting value for money? 95
- Payback period explained 95
- Payback period calculated 96
- Using payback period judiciously 98

Percent of Sales Method for Financial Forecasting 99
- Using sales to forecast future financial statements 99
- Percent of Sales Method explained 100
- Percent of Sales Method calculated 100
- The Drawback of the Percent of Sales Method 102

Profit Margin 103
- What your real profit is 103
- Profit Margin explained 103
- Profit Margin calculated 104
- Profit Margin interpreted 105
- Profit margin analysis application 105

Quick Ratio 107
- How liquid is your company? 107
- Quick Ratio explained 107
- Quick Ratio calculated 108
- Quick Ratio interpreted 109

Return on Total Assets 111
How effectively are your assets working for you? 111
ROTA explained 111
ROTA calculated 112
Further example 112
ROTA interpretation 113

Sales Mix Analysis 115
Mixing it up well to make the most of your sales 115
Sales Mix Analysis explained 115
Revenues 116
Sales Mix calculated 116
Sales Mix Analysis application 117

Sales per Person 119
How productive is your workforce? 119
Sales per Person explained 119
Sales per Person calculated 120
Sales per Person Ratio application 121
Conclusion 122

Sales to Current Assets Ratio 123
Leveraging current assets to generate sales 123
Sales to Current Assets Ratio explained 123
Sales to Current Assets Ratio calculated 124
Sales to Current Assets Ratio interpreted 125

Valuation of a Business 127
What's a business worth? 127
Asset Valuation Method 127
Sales Multiple Method 128
Earnings Multiple Method 128
Discounted Cash Flow Analysis..129
Buyer beware 129

Variable Cost to Fixed Cost 131
What's different, what's the same? 131
Variable and fixed cost explained 131
Variable and fixed costs calculated 132
Variable to fixed cost relationships 134
Variable and fixed cost summarized...134

Vertical Analysis..137
An apples-to-apples comparison tool 137
Vertical Analysis explained..137
Vertical Analysis calculated...138
Vertical Analysis–other uses 140

Volume (Denominator) Variance..143
Measuring production facilities...143
Volume (Denominator) Variance explained..............................143
Volume (Denominator) Variance calculated 144
Volume (Denominator) Variance interpreted............................146

Warehouse Cost Variances..147
What unchecked storage costs mean 147
Warehouse costs explained 147
Warehouse Cost Variances calculated........................148
Warehouse Cost Variances interpreted......................149

Working Capital 151
Liquidity when you need it..151
Working capital explained 151
Working capital calculated 152
Working capital application..153

Z-Score Model 155
Forecasting business failures 155
Z-Score Model explained..155
Z-Score Model Formulas 156
Z-Score Model example 157
Z-Score Model analysis 158

Conclusion 161

Acknowledgements

This book could not be possible without the support and love of the following people.

First are my grandparents, Joseph and Helen Takacs, who were Hungarian immigrants to America. Joseph and Helen built a great life and created a family with a strong work ethic and family values. All five of their sons, spouses, and grandchildren would have regular Sunday family dinners with them throughout the years. Although Joseph and Helen have passed, our family still comes together regularly for dinners, parties, and celebrations.

Support also came from my other grandmother, Jane Greenup, whose family came to America in the mid-1600s. Helen taught me how to understand and embrace the outdoors. She taught me how to fish, hunt, and use nature to heal ailments.

Next are my parents, Rudy and Nell Takacs, who raised my four younger sisters and me with the same values my grandparents instilled in all of us. And I cannot explain how blessed I am to have my four amazing sisters, Terri, Janet, Debra, and Laura. They have always been by my side as guiding and loving forces.

My sons, Chris and Greg, who always bring me joy and the ability to be a kid and skip along with them or just sit and play. Darn, they became men! Ah, but then there are the grandkids! Thank you, my sons.

Of course, my wife Dinia Takacs. We went from next-door neighbors to eventual husband and wife.

From the first evening that we celebrated her birthday as friends and the moonlit walk to our homes next door to one other in a small beach community, we have continued to grow our love and commitment to each other. This has been and continues to be a beautiful relationship. Dinia has been a loving wife who has supported my wild ventures in entrepreneurism.

My uncles, aunts, outlaws (my sister's spouses), cousins, nieces, nephews, and grandkids: these people have made me who I am today.

Now, my personal board of directors. This is my CEO University® group, a peer advisory board made up of CEOs from different industries. We come together to share our collective knowledge, resolve our issues, and capture opportunities while utilizing our knowledge-based solutions. They also keep me accountable (that is, kick my ass as needed).

I would like to thank Richard Warner, a CPA and partner at Smith Dickson, a certified public accounting firm, for his valuable input into this book.

Finally, my book team: Monty, Eliza, Teddi, and Megan for their expertise in this book's creation.

Introduction

When I started my career, I was working for our family business, oilfield equipment cutting tools. We were a design and manufacturing company in Houston, Texas. My father and each of my four uncles brought a variety of expertise to the company. Engineering design, production, manufacturing, finance, and sales. I was blessed to have had the opportunity as an apprentice, rotating around various functional areas of the company, and learning their area of expertise. Eventually, my family sold the company and shortly after the sale, I left to start my own firm in the same line of business. I did not have a non-compete agreement, since I did not own any of the family business.

Fortunately, there was still an oil boom going on in the world, and I was really good at engineering design, production, manufacturing, and sales. Accounting and finance–not so much! As my company, Tooling Technologies, Inc. grew, I realized just looking at the checkbook as a gauge for my business was not the right approach. I could not understand why the company accounts did not grow as fast as my company was growing–or did not grow at all! I did not realize that by growing rapidly, hiring more personnel, carrying more raw material, carrying more finished goods inventory, and buying more capital equipment to meet the demand, I was growing myself broke. I didn't heed the warning signs!

Though my CPA gave me my financials, I just was not smart enough to say, "I do not know what these statements mean." What the heck? I had money in the bank! I knew my jobs were extremely profitable, my customers loved us, so why was I in a cash crunch?

I finally told my CPA I had no idea what the statements I was getting meant and couldn't understand why I was in a cash crunch. That is when I learned of the power of financial metrics to guide your decision and business. And it is also my motivation to write this book.

From the embracing of financial metrics in my CEO toolbox, I was able to grow my business properly, profitably, and eventual sell my business. I went on to run companies in almost every industry utilizing *CEO Toolbox—Essentials for Success*®. This CEO Toolbox is also one pillar of CEO University, and we use this in all our CEO and Key Executive Peer Advisory Boards.

By the end of this book, I hope to give you the same knowledge and confidence that I received from using these KPIs. The information in this book and its accompanying KPI worksheet / workbook are all the resources you need to produce your personalized CEO playbook. Use them wisely and you too can keep your finger on the pulse of your business with early warning signs to help you turn things around quickly.

Accounts Payable Turnover Ratio

How do you pay your suppliers?

Accounts payable describes accounts that are established for goods and services which a company purchases. When the company buys items for business use, the good or services are paid with cash or billed to an account the company has established. It is common for suppliers to establish in-house accounts that are billed to the business on a monthly basis. Accounts payable can be paid in a few days to a few months, depending on the terms and agreements that are established with the affected vendors.

Accounts Payable Turnover Ratio explained

The Accounts Payable Turnover Ratio provides a measurable calculation or ratio that represents how the company pays its suppliers. The calculation is made by taking the total amount of purchases over a period of time and dividing it by the average accounts payable over the same time period.

The total supplier purchases will include all purchases made by the company over a set period of time, regardless of how the goods or services were paid.

Average accounts payable is the average amount owed to all suppliers over the same time period.

Accounts Payable Turnover Ratio calculated

$$\text{Accounts Payable Turnover} = \frac{\text{Total Supplier Purchases}}{\text{Average Accounts Payable}}$$

If the company maintains an inventory, this will require an adjustment in the Cost of Sales calculation. This would look like this:

Purchases = Cost of Sales + Ending Inventory – Starting Inventory

Using this adjustment to the purchases will offset the inventory that has been purchased and not yet sold, creating a more accurate calculation for purposes of the Turnover Ratio.

This ratio is most often calculated annually to establish how quickly the company pays for operating supplies. The ratio is tracked over time to see how one period compares to another as well as compared to other companies in the same industry. For example, if in a one-year period, a company purchases $100,000 in supplies, and the average accounts payable is $20,000, then the formula looks like this:

$$\text{Accounts Payable Turnover} = \frac{\$100{,}000}{\$20{,}000} = \text{A Ratio of 5}$$

Accounts Payable Turnover Ratio application

Comparing the ratio from one period to the next will help the company and investors see if they are taking longer to pay bills, or paying suppliers in a shorter period of time. It is a measure of outgoing payments.

For investors, the Accounts Payable Turnover Ratio is a measure of short-term liquidity. In other words, does the company have the cash to pay bills for company operations quickly and efficiently? A higher accounts payable ratio may also be an indication that the company is not being offered favorable payment terms with their current suppliers. This can affect cash flow significantly if sales are seasonal or fluctuate from month to month. Generally, a lower ratio is better than a higher one.

Accounts Receivable Turnover Ratio

Are your debtors a safe bet?

Every business, especially in the SME (small to medium enterprise) space, must extend credit to its customers if they wish to survive and thrive in today's highly competitive business environment. Sadly, what may be standard business practice in a particular industry (i.e., selling on credit), could be the death blow for some businesses if customers don't pay on time.

It is vital that business owners keep a close watch over the level and quality of the credit they extend to their business partners. The Accounts Receivable Turnover Ratio helps you do just that!

Accounts Receivable Turnover explained

The Accounts Receivable Turnover Ratio is an efficiency ratio that measures how effectively a business churns its credit sales (accounts receivable) in a given period and turns it into cash. By calculating this ratio, businesses can:

- assess whether they are extending sufficient credit facilities to their business partners

- analyze whether the company is doing a good job of collecting the amounts due to them

As a measure of efficiency, the Accounts Receivable Turnover Ratio can shed light on whether a company is (justly or unduly) doing business on a cash basis, or whether it has a sound and effective credit policy.

Accounts Receivable Turnover calculated

The Accounts Receivable Turnover Ratio measures the efficiency of a business's use of its accounts receivable. It is calculated using the formula:

$$\text{Accounts Receivable Turnover} = \frac{\text{Net Credit Sales}}{\text{Average Accounts Receivable}}$$

When calculating the numerator, allowances such as sales returns and other sales adjustments are deducted from credit sales figures to get net credit sales.

The denominator for this ratio is calculated as the averages between the opening and closing balances of accounts receivable during a period.

Let's assume the following partial data is from the balance sheet and income statements of XYZ Widget Company:

XYZ Widget Company		
Opening Accounts Receivable		$45,000
Closing Accounts Receivable		$15,000
Average Accounts Receivable = (A+B)/2		$30,000

XYZ Widget Company		
Gross Credit Sales	$110,000	
Sales Return	$35,000	
Net Credit sales = (D - E)		$75,000
Accounts Receivable Turnover = F/C		2.50

As indicated earlier, the Average Accounts Receivable balance is calculated by adding the opening and closing balances, and dividing the sum by 2.

The Net Credit Sales figure is calculated by subtracting Sales Returns ($35,000) from Gross Sales ($110,000), arriving at a Net Credit Sales figure of $75,000.

Using this data, and plugging the results into the formula, we get an Accounts Receivable Turnover of 2.5 (=$75,000/$30,000).

Accounts Receivable Turnover interpreted

Generally, higher ratios are preferable because they show that the company is efficient enough to collect its receivables more quickly, and then use that money to generate additional revenue/profitability for the business.

Let's use the above example to demonstrate what this means. As the data currently stands, of the $45,000 in Accounts Receivable that XYZ Widget Company had at the start of the period (plus new balance of Net Credit Sales $75,000 added during the period), $15,000 remains uncollected. So what does that mean for the company?

- That $15,000 is effectively "useless" for the company.
- It amounts to a "free loan" that the company has given to its business partners.

Accounts Payable Turnover Ratio

How soon do you pay?

In your personal life, when you buy an item using your credit card, you can rest assured that (depending on what your payment cycle is) your account will be debited on a specific date. Whether the date is 2 days or 21 days from placing your order, you'll pay the full amount that you owe.

Not so when it comes to business transactions. How you settle your accounts payable (the amount owed by you to your suppliers/business partners) might well determine whether you are better off or worse off for making payments earlier or later than you currently do. And the Accounts Payable Turnover Ratio can help you determine that.

Accounts Payable Turnover Ratio explained

Accounts Payable Turnover is a ratio that assesses how quickly (or slowly) a business pays its vendors (contractors, suppliers, consultants etc.).

Your vendors often propose varying payment terms when they quote you for products or services. Some of those terms may include clauses like:

- 1.5% discount if you pay the invoice immediately
- .5% discount if you pay within 5 days
- 1% interest (or late payment penalty) if you pay after the due date

Interestingly enough, business owners can use these terms to their advantage by running various scenarios and calculating their Accounts Payable Turnover Ratio. A declining turnover ratio from one period to another means you are paying your accounts payable more slowly than previously. Increasing ratios indicate quicker clearing of your dues.

Accounts Payable Turnover Ratio calculation

To calculate your Accounts Payable Turnover ratio, you can use the following formula:

$$\frac{\text{Total Credit Purchases During the Period}}{(\text{Opening Balance of Accounts Payable} + \text{Closing Balance of Accounts Payable})/2}$$

It is important to note that you are only analyzing *credit* purchases. Therefore, any payments by cash should be omitted from both the numerator and the denominator.

What this formula tries to highlight is the ratio of your credit purchases versus the average balance of credit purchases during the period under review.

For example, the XYZ Widget Company made credit purchases worth $300,000 during the period. The opening balance of Accounts Payable for the company was $475,000, and the closing balance of Accounts Payable was $520,000.

$$\text{Accounts Payable Turnover Ratio}$$
$$= \$300,000 / \{(\$475,000 + \$520,000)/2\}$$
$$= \$300,000 / \$497,500$$
$$= 0.60$$

The company's accounts payable have turned over 0.60 times during the period being reviewed.

Assuming that the company had an Accounts Payable Turnover Ratio of 1.20 in the last period, the declining (0.60) ratio this period indicates a slowdown in paying supplier invoices. Conversely, if the last period's ratio was 0.30, then the Current Ratio of 0.60 seems to indicate an increased pace of paying off Accounts Payable.

A common error to avoid

Some companies may use the Cost of Goods Sold (COGS) in place of total credit purchases as the numerator. Doing so will distort the Accounts Payable Ratio because COGS contains various other components (e.g., selling, general, administrative expenses) that are not directly related to Accounts Payable.

Accounts Payable Turnover Ratio application

On the face of it, this ratio (either declining or increasing in trend) doesn't tell us anything more than the fact that the pace of clearing credit purchase invoices (accounts payable) has reduced or accelerated. However, business managers must look deeper into the causes of such trends in order to really take advantage of what the ratio is telling us.

For instance:

- Did we increase the pace of making payments because suppliers are forcing us (by threatening to stop supplying us) to pay quicker? If so, that's a "bad" development.

- Did we start paying more quickly because we are now taking advantage of great credit terms (pay early and get purchase discounts)? If so, that's a "good" development.

- Are we paying later and maybe losing out on purchase discounts? That could be "good" or "bad" depending on whether the discounts are significant in terms of other uses of our cash.

- Are we forced to pay our bills late because we are facing a liquidity problem? That's a "bad" development.

- Has the ratio changed simply because we are now getting better credit terms? If so, then that's "good."

As a business owner, you need to keep track of your Accounts Payable Turnover Ratio, and monitor it over many periods to see what the trends are saying. Then, if you don't like the trends, you should dig deeper to assess whether the ratio results from "good" developments or "bad" ones.

In summary, you should use the ratio to ensure that your suppliers are paid within a reasonable timeframe: not too early so that you have to divert cash from other more productive uses, and not too late to miss out on possible purchase discounts or risk damaging your business relationships.

Asset Utilization Ratio

Utilizing assets efficiently

As an entrepreneur or business owner, you likely have a sizeable amount of your capital invested in business assets. They might be motor vehicles, plant and machinery, or high-tech computerized process control equipment. And as an investor, you'd like to know whether your assets are pulling their weight in making your business productive.

Read on to learn about the best way to know whether your business assets are working hard—and productively—just as you are!

You may own the latest and most cutting-edge assets amongst your peers and still not be as profitable as them. Why? Because you may not be using your assets as efficiently as your competitors are using theirs! And that competitiveness in asset use is measured by a ratio called the Asset Utilization Ratio.

Asset Utilization Ratio explained

Simply put, the Asset Utilization Ratio is a measure of management's aptitude to make the most efficient use of company assets to produce revenue. It evaluates how well assets are able to contribute in producing revenue. Just as Human Resources staffing becomes a drain on profitability when not used effectively, so too inefficiently used company assets can be a drag on productivity.

Asset Utilization Ratio calculated

Asset Utilization Ratio is a ratio between a company's revenue over the net book value of its assets. It is calculated as follows:

$$\frac{\text{Revenue for a Period}}{\text{Average Net Book Value of Capital Assets During the Period}}$$

Assume revenue for 2014 was $300,000 and Net Book Value of assets was $500,000, then the Asset Utilization Ratio would be:

$$\frac{\$300,000}{\$500,000} = \$0.60$$

Asset Utilization Ratio interpreted

In the example above, we calculated Asset Utilization as being 60 cents (or 60%). This means the company was able to earn 60 cents in revenue for every dollar of capital assets owned. If that ratio was 45% in 2013, it means asset utilization in 2014 has improved (assuming Book Value was the same).

Ideally, one is looking for an Asset Utilization Ratio that is on the higher end of a spectrum. The higher the ratio, the better assets are being utilized. However, "higher" might not always be ideal. Sometimes, by over utilizing assets, you might earn higher revenue from them, which will result in a higher Asset Utilization Ratio. But is that good for the assets?

Asset Utilization Ratio application

By frequently measuring Asset Utilization and comparing it against the ratios generated in prior periods, business owners will get a sense of how well their assets are working for them over time. Additionally, if you compare your Asset Utilization Ratio against your peer businesses, competitors or industry as a whole, you should be able to measure how well (or poorly) your assets are being utilized against comparative benchmarks.

A word of caution is in order. Revenue versus Asset Book Value should not be used in isolation when comparing asset efficiency. The age of the equipment, the technology behind the asset, the training received by operators, and operating conditions should also be considered in the assessment. However, the Asset

Bad Debt Ratio

As a businessperson, you rely on receiving revenue that you collect for products or services provided to your customers/clients. Unfortunately, a very important part of doing business involves extending credit (Accounts Receivable) to your customers, which means you don't get paid immediately for your goods/services. And sadly, sometimes, you might not get paid at all!

In simple terms, when your debtors (clients who owe you money) fail to pay you, you incur a bad debt.

Managing your debtors efficiently

Savvy customers will always try to press you (their supplier) for excessively liberal credit terms. And if you can't meet their requests (someone else may!), you may even end up losing a few clients. As a savvy business owner, the trick however is to ensure that you strike a delicate balance between extending appropriate credit to your customers, while also managing to collect against the debts they owe you.

Businesses can use the Bad Debt Ratio to assess whether they are doing a good job of managing outstanding receivables from their clients/customers.

Bad Debt Ratio explained

When you have a portion of your credit sales get into a state where they are unlikely to be collected (from your customers), they must be treated as a bad debt. Ultimately, after making diligent efforts to collect them, you will end up writing those debts off as a loss in your profit-and-loss statement.

Bad Debt Ratios are used to measure the percentage of such "uncollectable" debts, versus several other metrics, such as Sales or Accounts Receivable.

Bad Debt Ratio calculated

Depending on what metrics a business owner is trying to measure, we can calculate Bad Debt Ratios using either of two denominators: Accounts Receivable or Sales.

Bad Debt-to-Accounts Receivable Ratio

This ratio is the most commonly used variant for analyzing bad debt, and is calculated:

$$\frac{\text{Bad Debt}}{\text{Accounts Receivable}}$$

Assuming that a company extended credit to its clients totaling $100,000, and $2,000 of that amount was uncollectible, the Bad Debt-to-Accounts Receivable Ratio would be:

$$\$2,000 / \$100,000 \text{ or } 2\%$$

Bad Debt-to-Sales Ratio

Businesses may sometimes like to use a variant of the above ratio, using sales as the denominator. This is calculated:

$$\frac{\text{Bad Debt}}{\text{Sales}}$$

Assuming that a company made sales to its clients totaling $300,000, and $2,000 of that amount was uncollectible, the Bad Debt-to-Sales Ratio would be:

$$\$2,000 / \$300,000 \text{ or } 1\%$$

Bad Debt Ratio interpreted

A good rule of thumb for businesses to remember is the lower a Bad Debt Ratio is, the better it is for a business!

Referring to our first example above, in the case of the Bad Debt-to-Accounts Receivable Ratio, what it means is that, for every $100 worth of Credit Sales (or Accounts Receivable) extended to customers; $2 of it could not be collected.

In our second example, the Bad Debt-to-Sales Ratio, what it means is that, for every $100 worth of sales (both cash and credit) made to customers; $1 of it could not be collected.

Bad Debt Ratio application

We should not examine these Bad Debt Ratios in isolation. For instance, assume for a moment that both of the ratios in our examples relate to the same company, ABC Ltd. Further, assume that ABC Ltd. had the following transactions during the review period:

- Credit Sales $100,000
- Cash Sales $200,000
- Total Sales $300,000
- Bad Debts $2,000

If we went by the rule of thumb highlighted earlier, we'd probably be lulled into a false state of bliss thinking a 1% Bad Debt Ratio (Example 2) is better than a 2% Bad Accounts Receivable Ratio (Example 1). The truth of the matter is that, upon deeper inspection, we'll find that no matter how we slice/dice these results, we still lost 2% of our credit sales!

The point of using two different metrics to evaluate bad debt is to provide business owners/managers a sense of how effective their credit management policies are, and how efficient their cash management policies are. Bad Debt Ratios can be used to predict how credit worthy your clients are, and they can also be used to give you a sense of the provisions you need to make, in your balance sheet, to deal with them.

While being able to prove (through numbers) that the company collects $99 out of every $100 worth of sales is a good thing, it is alarming to see (in the numbers) that the company is unable to collect $2 out of each $100 worth of credit sales.

Both these ratios belong to the same family of ratios, yet they can be used to provide two different perspectives on the company's performance.

Cash Flow Ratios

Do you know how much accessible cash you need available to pay upcoming expenses?

An analysis of cash flow is useful for short-run planning. A firm needs cash to pay its debt maturing in the near future, to pay interest, to pay other expenses and to pay dividends to the shareholders. The firm can make projections of cash inflow and outflow for the near future to determine availability of cash. This cash balance can be matched with the firm's need for cash during that period, and arrangements can be made to meet the deficit or invest the surplus cash temporarily. A historical analysis of cash flow provides insight to prepare reliable cash flow projections for the immediate future.

Cash Flow Ratios explained

A statement of changes in financial position on *cash basis*, commonly known as cash flow statement, summarizes the causes of changes in cash position between the dates of two balance sheets. It indicates the sources and uses of cash. Cash flow statement is similar to fund flow statement except that it focuses attention on cash rather than working capital. The statement analyses changes in non-current accounts as well as current accounts to determine the flow of cash.

Cash Flow Ratios are important management accounting ratios that relate cash from operations or operating cash with other dynamics of business operation to judge solvency and liquidity of the company and also efficiency of the management in generating cash. Some of the Cash Flow Ratios and their significance are listed below.

Operating Cash Flow Ratio calculation

The Operating Cash Flow ratio is the relationship between cash from operation and current liabilities. It shows how the cash is accrued to current debts. It is a measure of liquidity as cash and current debts are related.

> Operating Cash Flow Ratio = Cash from Operation/Current Liabilities

Operating cash flow of less than 1 means the cash generated by the firm is not sufficient even to meet its current obligations. If the situation worsens, the firm may even go into liquidation.

Cash Flow Margin calculation

Cash Flow Margin is the ratio between cash from operations and net sales. The margin shows how much cash is generated in support of the sales. A high margin indicates the customers are maintaining a good and steady payment schedule, whereas a low ratio means a large part of the sales consist of book debts.

> Cash Flow Margin = (Cash from Operation/Net Sales) × 100

Price-to-Cash Ratio

The ratio shows the relationship between price per share and cash from operation per share. It is a better index than EPS (earnings per share) in determining the worth of the company because it emphasizes upon cash generation. Judging from the company's solvency point of view and ability to pay dividend, it is certainly better than simple earning because whole of the earning might not be realized.

Price/Cash Flow Ratio = Price per Share/Cash from Operation per Share

Cash Flow Solvency

The ratio is the relationship between cash from operations and total liabilities. It shows how much cash is there to support 1 dollar of liabilities. In other words, what is the cash coverage of liabilities? The higher the ratio, the greater the company's ability to pay off liabilities.

Cash Flow Solvency = Cash from Operations / Total Liabilities

Cash Flow Return on Assets

The Cash Flow ROA (Return on Assets) is the ratio between cash from operations and total assets employed. The ratio shows how efficiently the assets are being used to generate cash. The higher the ratio, the better the utilization of assets.

Cash Flow ROA = Cash from Operations / Total Assets Employed

	Company Corp Balance Sheet	
	31.03.2014	31.03.2013
	$	$
ASSETS		
Cash	126000	114000
Marketable securities	42400	20000
Debtors	60000	50000
Stock	38000	28000
Long term investments	28000	44000
Machinery	200000	140000
Buildings	240000	80000
Land	14000	14000
Total	748400	490000
LIABILITIES & EQUITY		
Accumulated depreciation	110000	60000
Creditors	40000	30000
Bills payable	20000	10000
Mortgage loan	200000	100000
Share capital	220000	160000
Share premium	24000	nil
Reserve & surplus	134400	130000
Total	748400	490000
Number of equity shares	25000	25000
Price per share	$4	$4

Company Corp
Income Statement 2013

	$	$
Sales		240000
Cost of goods sold		134800
Gross profit		105200
Less: Operating expenses		
Depreciation – Machinery	20000	
Depreciation - Building	32000	
Other expenses	40000	92000
Net profit from operation		13200
Gain on sale of long term investment		4800
Total		18000
Loss on sale of machinery		2000
Net profit		16000

Solution
Company Corp Cash Flow Ratios

		$						
	Net profit	16000						
	Add:							
	Depreciation - Machinery	20000						
	Depreciation - Building	32000						
	Loss on sale of machinery	2000						
	Increase in creditors	10000						
	Increase in bills payable	10000	90000					

			Less:					
	Gain on sale of long term investment		4800					
	Increase in debtors		10000					
	Increase in stock		10000	24800				
	Cash from operations			65200				
	Cash from operations per share		[65200/	2.608				
			25000]					
	Price per share			4				
	Ratios							
1	Operating cash flow ratio		Cash from operation/		65200/60000		1.086667	
			Current liabilities					
2	Cash flow margin		(Cash from operations/		(65200/240000) x 100		27.16667	
			Net sales)100	x 100			(%)	
3	Price to cash ratio		Price per share/Cash from		4/2.608		1.533742	
			operations per share					
4	Cash flow solvency		[Cash for operations/		[65200/		0.087119	
			total liabilities]		748400]			
5	Cash from ROA		[Cash from operations/		[65200/		14.36123	
			to total fixed assets employed]		454000]x100		(%)	

Current Ratio

What is the proportion of current assets to current liabilities?

The Current Ratio is a short-term liquidity ratio that assists in identifying the organization's ability to meet working capital needs within 12 months. This includes current liabilities (those liabilities that are due to be settled within 12 months), which are to be covered by its current assets (those assets that are to be realized within 12 months).

Current Ratio explained

If the Current Ratio is 2, then this means the current assets are adequate to cover twice the amount of the organizations current liabilities. Minimum Current Ratio levels are usually placed in loan covenants and are used to protect the interest of the lenders from deteriorating financial position. Even various countries have placed financial regulations on Current Ratio demands with regard to offering loans.

Current Ratio calculated

$$\text{Current Ratio} = \frac{\text{Current Assets}}{\text{Current Liabilities}}$$

XYZ Balance Sheet as of 31st December 2014:

	$	$
Non-Current Assets		
Fixed Assets	70	70
Current Assets		
Cash in hand	40	
Inventory	30	
Cash in bank	20	
Receivable	60	150
Current Liabilities		
Trade Payables	90	
Other Short Term Liabilities	40	130
Non-Current Liabilities		
Long Term Loan	50	
Other Long Term Liabilities	20	70
Shareholder Equity	20	20

The Current Ratio of XYZ is as follows:

$$\text{Current Ratio} = \frac{\text{Current Assets}}{\text{Current Liabilities}} = \frac{150}{130} = 1.15$$

The XYZ Company has a Current Ratio of 1.15, which shows the company is covering its working capital needs with a minimum cushion.

Current Ratio interpreted

Interpretation and analysis of Current Ratio by the business should be based on the following:

- Analysis of Current Ratio trends must be done regarding the industry standard in which the organization operates.

- The Current Ratio should be monitored over a period.

- The organization should target a Current Ratio of minimum 1 because this ensures that the current assets are at least covering their short-term obligations.

- A Current Ratio greater than 1 provides the organization with an additional cushion for unforeseeable contingencies, which may arise in the short-term period.

- A Current Ratio of less than 1 is a sign that the company might not cover its working capital needs.

- A Current Ratio that is much higher than industry standard is not a good sign. Instead, it shows inefficient use of resources because it shows that working capital is not being used for more profitable purposes. Similarly, a Current Ratio lower than industry standard is a sign of a risky strategy and could cause liquidity issues for the business.

- A continuous increasing trend in Current Ratio over a specific timeframe is either a sign of improved liquidity or conservative approach being taken up by the business with regard to working capital management. A continuous decreasing trend in Current Ratio over a specific timeframe is either a sign of a deteriorating liquidity position or a leaner approach to the working capital cycle for the business.

- When studying Current Ratio trends over a specific timeframe, seasonal fluctuations need to be taken into considerations.

Current Liability Ratio

Determine your ability to settle short-term obligations

Businesses around the world depend on credit. They seek credit (take loans, buy goods on credit from suppliers) and they extend credit (perform services on credit for their clients, extend loans to customers). The liabilities that credit generates for a business are not necessarily a bad thing. However, for an enterprise to be successful, businesses must continually assess their ability to service those liabilities, especially in the short term.

The Current Ratio, also called the Working Capital Ratio, is a tool that helps a business to quickly ascertain whether it can service its short-term liabilities using current liquidity in the business.

Current Liability Ratio explained

According to Generally Acceptable Accounting Principles (GAAP), businesses must classify their assets and liabilities into two categories:

- current: those which are due within 1 accounting cycle (usually a year)
- long-term: those which are due beyond the current accounting cycle (usually more than a year out)

Current Liabilities, therefore, are those that will be due for settlement either within the current business cycle, or shortly thereafter. And since they are "current" by definition, a business must have the ability to settle them through "currently liquid" assets. A liability (for example, a bank loan) due is 1 month from today cannot be paid off by proceeds of a customer invoice due to be received in 6 months from today.

The Current Ratio is a measure of liquidity that demonstrates a business's ability to settle short-term liabilities using its current assets.

Current Liability Ratio calculated

The Current Liability Ratio is calculated using the following formula:

$$\frac{\text{Current Assets}}{\text{Current Liabilities}}$$

Assuming that a company has $100,000 in current assets, and $30,000 in current liabilities, the Current Ratio would be:

$$\$100,000 / \$30,000 \text{ or } 3.3$$

On the other hand, if the situation was reversed, and the company has $30,000 in current assets, and had accumulated $100,000 in current liabilities, the Current Ratio would be:

$$\$30,000 / \$100,000 \text{ or } 0.30$$

Both numerator (Current Assets) and denominator for this ratio are taken from the company's balance sheet.

Current Liability Ratio interpreted

Since, by definition, the Current Liability Ratio is a measure of how well (or poorly!) a business can apply current assets against current liabilities, the above examples tell us the following:

- In Example #1, the Current Liability Ratio is greater than 1. This means that for every $1 of current liabilities, the company has more than $1 ($3.30 in fact!) of current assets to cover the liabilities when they become due. Typically, this would be a good thing (more on this shortly).

- In Example #2, the Current Liability Ratio is less than 1. This means the company has less than a dollar (only 30 cents!) in currently liquid assets to pay off each dollar of liability that's currently coming due! And that is definitely a bad thing! If, by the time the liabilities come due, the company doesn't come up with adequate resources to pay them, it could result in financial challenges.

Typically, the higher the ratio, the better it is for a business. However, Current Liability Ratios should not be looked at in isolation. One has to look at the nature of the business and the industry that it is in to make a determination of whether the Current Liability Ratio is adequate or not. If every other competing business in an industry has a Current Liability Ratio of 1.5, then having a ratio of 4.5 or 6.0 might not be a good thing.

Current Liability Ratio application

This last statement may seem at odds to a previous statement: that higher Current Ratios are better. But it is not at odds. Why? Because a business should *not* just conserve its current assets (cash, short-term investments etc.) to pay off current liabilities. In a business environment where a Current Ratio of 1.5 is the norm, a 4.5 or 6.0 ratio might mean excessive hording of current assets, to the point that a business loses the opportunity to invest it for better returns.

Use the Current Liability Ratio to assess whether you have sufficient, but not overly excessive, ability to service your current liabilities.

The Current Liability Ratio has yet another use: to assess whether your customer/client is a potential credit risk. Use their Current Liability Ratio to ascertain, if you extend them a short-term credit facility, whether they will be able to repay you back using their current assets. A company that has working cash flow issues is unlikely to be able to service its short-term liabilities, and an analysis of their Current Liability Ratio will reveal that.

Days of Inventory Outstanding

How good are you at turning inventory into sales?

Continuous cash flow is to a business as unhindered blood flow is to the human body. Impeded in any way, blood flow can cause atrophy among our limbs, and may also lead to other serious health challenges. Likewise, when working capital is tied up in various aspects of the business, it can lead to major cash flow issues. And one of the most frequent culprits for those issues is an impeded flow of inventory out of your warehouses and stores. Days Inventory Outstanding (DIO) is a measure that indicates how well (or poorly) inventory flows through the organization.

DIO explained

DIO measures the average number of days that inventory is held within an organization before it moves off the shelves in the form of sales. The lower the DIO number, the better: it means cash is tied up for a shorter duration, and that inventory is turned over more quickly.

DIO is a key element in any business's cash conversion cycle, which is comprised of activities designed to turn key business processes, such as purchases, accounts payables, and accounts receivable, into cash.

DIO calculated

Days Inventory Outstanding (DIO) Formula
$$\frac{\text{Average Inventory Value}}{\text{Cost of Goods Sold}} \times \text{Number of days in review period}$$

The average inventory value and cost of goods sold relate to a period for which the DIO metric is to be calculated.

Let's assume your average inventory for the year (365 days) is $35,000, and that your cost of goods sold is $250,000.

Days Inventory Outstanding (DIO) Example
$$\frac{\$35{,}000}{\$250{,}000} \times 365$$
DIO = 51.1

Based on these assumptions, it takes you an average of 51 days to move your inventory off the shelves, and convert them into sales. Is that good or bad? We'll discuss the nuances shortly.

The other aspect of DIO relates to profitability and obsolescence factors.

The quicker your turnover (the rate of replenishing and selling) your inventory, the more profitable you'll be. And the longer that inventory remains within the company, the greater the risk of obsolescence (the inventory becoming "stale").

Monthly Inventory Profitability Scenarios		
	Scenario 1	Scenario 2
Value of inventory on hand	$100,000	$100,000
Profit margin	15%	15%
Sales revenue earned	$115,000	$115,000
Profit earned	**$15,000**	**$15,000**
Value of inventory on hand	$100,000	$100,000
Profit margin	15%	15%
Sales revenue earned	$0	$115,000
Profit earned	**$0**	**$15,000**
Total Profit earned	**$15,000**	**$30,000**

In the above two scenarios, if a company has a DIO of 30 days (selling inventory once in a month), it will convert inventory into cash just once per month, earning a profit of $15,000 every month (Scenario 1). A competitor (Scenario 2) who has a DIO of 15 days, on the other hand, moves their inventory twice during a month, therefore earns twice as much profit. Additionally, the $100,000 inventory left unsold (Scenario 1) is at risk of growing obsolete.

The nuances of DIO

Like most business metrics, DIO isn't free from its nuances. For instance, as a CEO, you may not be able to compare the DIO values of two segments of your business, and deem the one with the higher value inefficient. For instance, if Scenario 1 represented an art gallery, and Scenario 2 represented a grocery business, fast-moving fresh produce inventory must have lower DIO's than discretionary items, like artwork and paintings. So, business leaders must make apples-to-apples comparisons to come to meaningful conclusions using the DIO metric.

At the top of this post, we noted DIO was a critical element in managing cash flow. So, how can CEOs manage DIO? Well, there are a few viable strategies to do so, including:

- more efficient selling
- better marketing and branding
- offering more attractive/favorable pricing and payment terms

These, and other similar strategies, are meant to super-charge the movement of inventory off your shelves, and convert that investment (in stock) into cash flow as quickly as possible.

Days Sales Outstanding

How quickly do you collect payments once you make a sale?

Your money in your hands is worth more to you than if it's in someone else's bank account! If it's in your bank account, you control what you do with it. When it's just owed to you, someone else uses it to their advantage—possibly to your detriment! So how many days' worth of sales do you typically have, sitting with your customers once you've made a sale? That's exactly what Days Sales Outstanding (DSO) helps businesses figure out.

DSO explained

To put it succinctly, DSO is an accounting metric that evaluates the average number of days' sales that a company has tied up as accounts receivable. In other words: how many days of sales does your account receivables represent?

Viewed yet another way, how long does it take you to convert accounts receivable (i.e., *your* cash in *someone else's* hands) into cash (*your* cash in *your* hands).

Remember, DSO is not a measure of the effectiveness of your collection process. We use other metrics, such as AR Turnover Ratio or Average Days Delinquent to measure that function. DSO tells you the average of days' sales in the pipeline awaiting collection.

DSO calculated

Days Sales Outstanding (DSO) Formula		
$\dfrac{\text{Accounts Receivables}}{\text{Credit Sales during review period}}$	X	Number of days in review period

DSO application

Use DSO when:

1. Accounts receivables balance is the cumulative balance of your outstanding sales at the end of an assessment period.

2. Credit sales during a period represents the net new credit sales made for a period: a month, a quarter, 6 months, etc.

3. The number of days in the review period is 30, 60, 90, 120, or whatever window of time you choose. It must match the period representing the sales in the denominator.

For example, if you made $1.5 million worth of sales during the month and, at the end of the month, you had $300,000 worth of sales outstanding, your DSO would be 6.

Days Sales Outstanding (DSO) Example		
$\dfrac{\$300{,}000}{\$1{,}500{,}000}$	X	30
DSO	=	6

In simpler terms: $1.5 million in monthly sales translate into $50,000 sales daily. If you have $300,000 in sales outstanding at the end of the month, that's 6 days of equivalent sales ($50,000 × 6 = $300,000).

The nuances of DSO

It takes a steady inflow of revenue to fund your ongoing operations. Typically, companies with high DSO will likely experience cash flow challenges. However, the quality of DSO is relative. For instance, in agri-businesses, sales proceeds for inputs, such as fertilizer and seed, are typically collected at the end of a harvesting season. So, a 90- or 150-day DSO may be considered normal. For a professional services firm, however, like an architect or web designer, a 45- to 60-day DSO might be excessive. A food delivery business must collect in fewer than a matter of days, otherwise they may find it difficult to continue operations for too long.

Unusually high DSO values should also prompt you to review your credit sales policies. Perhaps they are too liberal: good for your customers, but detrimental to your own cash flow.

DSO might also give you an advance indication of the financial stability of your customers. An underlying reason that it takes you longer (compared to, say, a competitor) to convert sales into cash, might be that your clients can't service their debts easily. If that's the case, high DSO values may serve as a warning that you should try seeking alternative markets to serve.

When building cash flow planning models, it is important to factor your DSO into the model. If you work with investors, bankers, creditors, and external stakeholders, they typically view DSO as a measure of your effectiveness to convert receivables into cash flow, a metric that's critical for business operations.

Days of Working Capital

Convert capital to revenue more quickly

Business owners are often worried about the level of working capital they have on their balance sheets, "just to make ends meet"—and rightly so! The thinking is that you must have sufficient capital on hand to cover your current liabilities, those that are coming due in the short term. And that's a good thing.

Sometimes though, in trying to meet liquidity concerns, businesses forget about one other important measure of efficiency: the rate at which that working capital is turned back into revenue for the company. And that's where Days of Working Capital comes in.

Days of Working Capital explained

Working capital is what companies use to fund short-term liabilities using their current assets. It is calculated by subtracting current liabilities from current assets. After doing the math, what you are left with may be equated to fuel that keeps the wheels of your business turning.

Ideally, most companies would like to hoard a pile of cash in their banks to fuel business activity, "just in case." However, that would be a highly inefficient use of current assets (cash). Instead, an efficient business should have just enough working capital on hand that it can then turn it, in a reasonable amount of time, back into revenue (sales).

Days of Working Capital provides business owners a measure of the aforementioned reasonable amount of time in days. It tells you how many days it takes to convert working capital into revenue.

Days of Working Capital calculated

Looked at in a different light, Days of Working Capital may be seen as the interval (in days) between when you pay your bills for the cost of sales of your goods/services, and when you actually receive payment from customers to whom you sold those goods/services. It can be calculated using the following formula:

$$\text{Days Working Capital} = \frac{(\text{Average Working Capital} \times 365)}{(\text{Average Working Capital} \times 365)}$$

the average working capital used in the numerator is calculated by summing the opening and closing balances of working capital during the period, and dividing the result by 2 to get an average.

Let's look at an example using sample data from the XYZ Widget Company.

XYZ Widget Company		
Sample Data for Days Working Captial		
A	Working Captial (Current Year)	$260,000
B	Working Capital (Prior Year)	$180,000
C	Total Working Captial (= A + B)	**$440,000**
D	Average Working Capital (= C / 2)	$220,000
E	Sales Revenue	$25,000,000
F	Days Working Capital	**3.21**

The first step in the calculation (C) yields a total working capital of $440,000, which is averaged out (D) to get $220,000.

Next, when we multiply the average working capital (D) by 365, we get $80,300,300 (not shown here) which, when divided by the sales revenue (E) gives us a figure of 3.21 days (F).

This is the number of days that it takes XYZ Widget Company to change its working capital into actual revenue.

Days of Working Capital interpreted

Ideally, business owners should be pleased with a lower Days of Working Capital, because it signals that the company is turning working capital into sales revenue quickly. In the above instance, a ratio of, say, 2.5 days would be much better than the current 3.21 days, and a ratio of 5.25 days would be something to shun.

Having said that however, as with all other fundamental analysis tools, the Days of Working Capital must be interpreted in certain perspective. Each business in every industry might have qualifying factors that lend different interpretations of this metric.

Measuring the Days of Working Capital of clothing retailers (which usually have short turnover cycles) for instance, against that of airplane manufacturers (which have exceptionally long turnover cycles) is not appropriate. Such a comparison will be meaningless, because the working capital requirement for each of those industries is starkly different.

Additionally, Days of Working Capital should always be analyzed in comparison to prior periods. An unfavorable ratio in Period 2 (versus Period 1) should be investigated for underlying causes. If the ratio is used in isolation, without prior-period comparison, business owners may not be able to do root-cause analysis to locate and fix the reasons for the degradation of its Days Working Capital metric.

Depreciation

The act of writing-down assets

It is a known fact that any piece of equipment, be it a car, an airplane, an oil refining plant, or a packing machine, can only serve its purpose for so long. Business owners can initiate clever maintenance routines, but that will only serve a limited purpose. Eventually, the asset gradually loses its life (and value).

And that's precisely what accountants and finance professionals recognize in a company's fixed assets: a state where the usefulness of an asset declines over time. As a result, Generally Accepted Accounting Principles (GAAP) mandates that accountants recognize that entropy. It even has a name. It's called depreciation.

Depreciation explained

Accounting allows us to allocate the cost of an asset's depreciation using two broad methods:

1. Based on the time that the asset is used. This category of depreciation can be calculated using three variations of a similar formula.

    a. Straight-Line

    b. Declining Balance

    c. Sum-of-the-Year's Digit

2. Based on the amount (activity) of usage.

Most federal/state regulators allow a company to select the method they want to use to recognize depreciation on their assets, but there may be industry-standards that govern individual depreciation choices.

Use Case Depreciation Formula

Purchase date	: April 1, Year 1
Asset Cost	: $140,000.
Useful Life (estimated)	: 5 years (making the rate of depreciation 1/5 = 20% per year)
Salvage value	: $20,000.

Straight-Line Depreciation Formula

$$\frac{(\text{Asset Cost} - \text{Residual Value})}{\text{Useful Life}}$$

Year 1 Depreciation (for .75% of the year, April–December)

= {($140,000 − $20,000) × .75} × 20% = $18,000

Year 2 Depreciation (for the whole year, January–December)

= ($140,000 − $20,000) × 20% = $24,000

Declining Balance Depreciation Formula

The Declining Balance method does not consider residual value, and has three main components:

1. depreciation each period = book value × rate of depreciation
2. accumulated depreciation = sum of depreciation each period
3. asset's declining balance = book value − accumulated depreciation

The Declining Balance table for this scenario would look like this:

A	B	C	D	E	F	G	H
Year	Cost of Asset	Accumulated Depreciation at Start of year	Rate of Depreciation	Percentage of period	Depreciation for the year	Accumulated Depreciation at End of year	Declining Balance Book Value of Asset at End of year
					{(B-C)*D} × E	C+F	B-G
1	$140,000	$0	20%	75%	$21,000.00	$21,000.00	$119,000.00
2	$140,000	$21,000	20%	100%	$23,800.00	$44,800.00	$95,200.00
3	$140,000	$44,800	20%	100%	$19,040.00	$63,840.00	$76,160.00
4	$140,000	$63,840	20%	100%	$15,232.00	$79,072.00	$60,928.00
5	$140,000	$79,072	20%	100%	$12,185.60	$91,257.60	$48,742.40

In some cases, the depreciation for the year (column F) is calculated as declining balance of asset (H from previous year) minus depreciation

(F for current year). The result, of course, would be the same: the declining balance for the year would always work out to be in line with what's shown above, whether you use book value – depreciation or cost – accumulated depreciation.

For more heavily depreciated assets, there are also variations of the Declining Balance Method: double-declining balance, which uses twice the depreciation rate (e.g., 20% × 2 = 40%) or times-and-half declining balance (e.g., 20% × 1.5 = 30%).

Sum-of-the-Years' Digits Depreciation Formula

Sum-of-the-Years' Digits method uses a factor (or factorial) based on the sum of the number of years of the asset's expected life.

Use Case:

Purchase date: January 1, Year 1, Cost = $140,000, Residual Value = $20,000, Life = 5 years

In the use case above, since the asset life is 5 years, the denominator for the factor is: 1 + 2 + 3 + 4 + 5 = 15. The numerator for the first year is: n / denominator, where n is the life in years. The numerator for the second year is n-1; and for the fifth year it would be 1.

The depreciation table for this scenario would look like this:

Year	Cost	Residual Value	Depreciable Value	Factor	Depreciation Expense
1	$140,000	$20,000	$120,000	0.33	$40,000.00
2	$140,000	$20,000	$120,000	0.27	$32,000.00
3	$140,000	$20,000	$120,000	0.20	$24,000.00
4	$140,000	$20,000	$120,000	0.13	$16,000.00
5	$140,000	$20,000	$120,000	0.07	$8,000.00

Usage-Based Depreciation Formula

When it comes to calculating depreciation based on usage, the formula is simple:

1. Estimate how many products (or usage in terms of miles, hours, etc.) an asset is good for.
2. Divide the cost of the asset by that number to get a depreciation rate.
3. Each year, estimate (or record precisely) how many products (or miles, hours, etc.) the asset was used for.
4. Multiply that value by the depreciation rate.

Use Case

A truck was purchased for $140,000 with a salvage value of $20,000. It was estimated the truck would run for a maximum of 500,000 km.

The depreciation table for this use case would look like this:

A Year	B Cost	C Estimated usage (km)	D Residual Value	E Depreciable Value	F Depreciation Rate/km	G Actual Usage (km)	H Depreciation Expense
				(B-D)	(B/C)		(F*G)
1	$140,000	500,000	$20,000	$120,000	$0.28	55,000.00	$15,400.00
2	$140,000	500,000	$20,000	$120,000	$0.28	97,000.00	$27,160.00
3	$140,000	500,000	$20,000	$120,000	$0.28	110,000.00	$30,800.00
4	$140,000	500,000	$20,000	$120,000	$0.28	120,000.00	$33,600.00
5	$140,000	500,000	$20,000	$120,000	$0.28	45,000.00	$12,600.00

Depreciation application

While depreciation is grounded in the reality that all assets must expire someday, it also serves a very real financial purpose. Depreciation ensures that the full cost of an asset is not written off (expensed) all at once. Instead, since the asset will be useful, and will contribute to revenue over a period of time, accounting's Matching Principle mandates that expenditure incurred in earning such revenue be matched by expenditure in appropriate periods.

Depreciation formulas are therefore used to calculate a portion of expense to be matched against revenues in a given accounting period.

Fixed Asset Ratios

Assessing asset performance

Businesses depend on their fixed assets (such as plant and machinery, fleet of vehicles, communications equipment, drilling platforms, excavation machines, etc.) to generate revenue. And sometimes, when an enterprise is doing well, business owners don't take the time to assess how much of the good times are the result of their fixed assets.

One way to find out how your assets are performing, and whether they are truly assets or liabilities for the company, is with the help of Fixed Asset Ratios.

Fixed Asset Ratios explained

Fixed Asset Ratios analysis is a technique that accountants and financial analysts use to assess how a company's fixed assets are positioned against other key metrics of the company. All of this information is gleaned by combining information from the company's balance sheet and income statement.

The ratios so calculated are then used to drive various business decisions.

Fixed Asset Ratios calculated

There are several different flavors of Fixed Assets Ratios. Here are two of the most widely used of these ratios.

Fixed Assets to Net Worth Ratio

This is a ratio that seeks to measure how solvent (able to pay its debts) a company is. It gives analysts an assessment of the extent to which a company's capital is tied up in the form of fixed assets, including buildings and property, plant and equipment, and motor vehicles. In doing so, analysts can also assess how much working capital a company has left to run the company's day-to-day business operations.

$$\text{Fixed Assets to Net Worth Ratio} = \frac{\text{Net Fixed Assets}}{\text{Net Worth}}$$

Assuming a company's Net Worth (inclusive of all assets and investments) is $2,000,000, and its Fixed Assets (after depreciation) is $100,000, its Fixed Assets to Net Worth Ratio would be:

$$\frac{\$100,000}{\$2,000,000} \text{ or } 0.05$$

Generally speaking, a Fixed Assets to Net Worth Ratio below 0.75 is desirable, since that shows the company has adequate working capital protection to deal with any unforeseen operational issues.

Fixed Assets Turnover Ratio

This ratio analyzes the proportion of a company's sales revenue to its fixed assets. In doing so, analysts get a sense of how effective fixed assets are in churning out sales revenue. In other words, the Fixed Assets Turnover Ratio tells us how many dollars of revenue each dollar of assets brings in.

$$\text{Fixed Assets Turnover Ratio} = \frac{\text{Sales Revenue}}{\text{Total Fixed Assets}}$$

Assuming a company's sales revenue for the year is $200,000, and its total fixed assets (excluding special asset classes like goodwill and deferred taxes) is $100,000, its Fixed Asset Turnover Ratio would be:

$$\frac{\$200,000}{\$100,000} \text{ or } 2$$

This means that for every dollar invested in fixed assets, the company is earning $2 in return.

Generally speaking, Fixed Assets Turnover Ratios are compared on a year-to-year basis to see if the turnover increases over time. Even if the ratio is declining, that does not indicate anything negative, as aging fixed assets tend to be less productive over time. However, the pace at which the decline occurs must be investigated.

Fixed Asset Ratios application

By using a company's fixed assets as a yardstick, and comparing them to other metrics, analysts can figure out:

- what percentage of a company's financial position is represented by fixed assets
- whether the fixed assets are contributing (or hindering) profitability
- how well the company's fixed assets are being utilized

In addition to company-specific investment decisions (Should we invest more in Fixed assets? Should we cut down on in-efficient capital expenditure?), the Fixed Asset Ratios can assess how well a company's assets are performing against other industry peers.

For publicly traded corporations, Fixed Asset Ratios can provide valuable insight into managements' ability to use company assets effectively to drive shareholder return on investment (ROI). If the company produces poor ratios continually, investors will likely lose confidence in company management, divest their holdings, and invest elsewhere.

Gross Income Multiplier

Assessing rental property

Like any other business owner, entrepreneurs in the real estate business are always on the lookout for properties that will turn them a healthy profit. And sometimes, prospective buyers need to make quick decisions about the profitability of a transaction.

Whether one is buying the property outright or leasing it, if the deal doesn't look good as a result of "back of the napkin" calculations, then most investors will hesitate making a bid for the property.

Gross Income Multiplier explained

Gross Income Multiplier (GIM) formula is a quick, "back of the napkin," way to assess the profitability of a rental property. If you are eager to buy/lease a rental property, you'd like to see if doing so is worth the investment value. By enabling the calculation of the ratio between the price for the property and the estimated rental income expected from it, the GIM formula offers you a quick way to see if this is a worthy proposition.

GIM calculated

Assume that you want to purchase a two-unit rental tenement for $200,000, and you expect to receive $750 per month from each of the tenants. That would translate into rental income of $1,500 per month ($750 × 2) and $18,000 annually ($1,500 × 12).

Gross Income Multiplier Formula:

$$\frac{\text{Property Value}}{\text{Annual Income}}$$

$$\frac{\$200{,}000}{\$18{,}000} = 11 \text{ (approximately)}$$

This tells us that you will be paying 11 times the potential annual income for this property.

The GIM formula can be used to do some reverse engineering to estimate the value proposition between this property and others in the area. For instance, assume that there is another tenement in the vicinity that offers you the potential of $21,000 a year in rental income.

Since both properties are in the same neighborhood, we can reasonably use a slightly different variation of the GIM formula (GIM × annual income), to quickly come up with an estimated value for that second property: 11 × $21,000 = $231,000.

Investors can then use both sets of numbers to drive a decision for where to invest. If the actual value of Property #2 is higher, then based on a GIM result of 11, it would not be a worthwhile investment proposition.

GIM Formula application

While popularly used to assess the feasibility of a real estate (rental) deal, the GIM formula can be used as a generic measure to quickly establish the viability of other business transactions. For instance, assume that you are participating in an auction for previously owned heavy machinery. If a piece of equipment is selling for $100,000, and you believe it will net you $3,000 a month in revenue, should you make a bid for it?

The GIM formula would be:

$$\$100,000 / (\$3,000 \times 12) = 2.78$$

Using a GIM result of 2.78 (or 3, for rough decision-making purposes) tells you that you'll be paying 3 times the value of expected yearly revenue for it. Are you comfortable with roughly a 3-year payback? If so, you may want to quickly put in a bid. If not, you should look for another opportunity with a lower GIM.

GIM Formula limitations

At the outset of this article we made reference to "back of the napkin" calculations; and that's exactly what GIM is. It's a great tool to use when making quick comparisons. However, before one actually puts money into a property (or a piece of income-generating equipment), one needs to know more than just a price for the property/equipment and its estimated income generating capacity.

For instance, due diligence would mandate that you take into consideration factors like:

- maintenance costs
- utilities

- financing costs
- closing costs
- annual operating costs

None of these are taken into consideration when calculating the GIM formula, although they should be, because they affect the overall capital investment decision. However, one might counter that the GIM outcome is a good enough indicator to use by using the caveat of "other costs being equal…"

Gross Profit Variance

A great checkpoint for business performance

As a business prepares its financial statements–income statement, balance sheet, and cash flow statement–for the quarter or the end of the year, accountants and financial analysts glean valuable insight into how the business has performed during the review period. Using Gross Profit Variance is one way to make use of income statement data to assess a company's performance.

Gross Profit Variance explained

In simple terms, Gross Profit Variance analysis is a tool used to measure the company's gross profit against a multitude of metrics. These measurement metrics may be:

- Baseline data. For instance, the baseline may be the gross profit earned by the industry or specific competitors in the industry at a certain point in time.

- Budgeted data. This can analyze various components of gross profit (e.g., sales value or sales quantity) against budgeted (or planned) values.

- Standards data. For instance, the analysis of the amount of scrap, spoilage, or rejects produced.

- Historical data. This is used to compare gross profit for the current period against prior periods or the prior 3, 5, or 10 years.

The analysis seeks to measure how the current period's gross profit squares off against any or all of these comparators. If there is a difference, negative or positive, it highlights what that difference is.

Gross Profit Variance calculated

The calculation of the Gross Profit Variance involves two distinct phases. The first step relates to deciding on the comparator. For instance, most variances are compared against prior periods, so the accountant or analyst must determine how many periods to use and which ones.

Once that's decided, the gross profit for those comparator years must be made available for the variance calculation.

Next, the Gross Profit Variance for the current period must be calculated using the following formula:

$$\text{Gross Profit for Current Period} = \text{Current Period Sales} - \text{Direct Materials Consumed} - \text{Direct Labor Used} - \text{Manufacturing Overheads}$$

Now that both elements for the variance analysis are available, the Gross Profit Variance can be calculated:

$$\text{Gross Profit Variance} = \text{Gross Profit for Current Period} - \text{Gross Profit Comparator}$$

The result may indicate a positive (good) or a negative (bad) variance.

For instance, assuming that we are conducting a Gross Profit Variance analysis for Q2 of 2015, where Gross profit was $210,000. Gross profit for Q1, 2015 was $195,000, and that for Q2, 2014 was $317,000.

One way to conduct a Gross Profit Variance analysis would be:

Gross Profit Q2, 2015	Gross Profit Last Period (Q1, 2015)	Gross Profit Variance (This Period v. Last Period)	Gross Profit Percentage Variance	Gross Profit Same Period Last Year (Q2 2014)	Gross Profit Variance (v. Same Period Last Year)	Gross Profit Percentage Variance
$210,000	$195,000	$15,000	8%	$317,000	-$107,000	-34%

Instead of value, the above table could have included units of measure (e.g., number of products sold, or hours of service rendered). Many analysts prefer to see both elements (value and quantity) side-by-side.

Because of this assessment we can see that the company has produced operational performance that's 8% better this period compared to its last quarter. However, on a year-over-year basis, the company has done rather poorly, with Gross profit trending downwards by a whopping 34%.

So, what does this mean?

Gross Profit variances can be caused by several factors, including:

- changes to the sale price of products/services
- variance in the number of units of product/service sold
- variation in the product/service mix sold
- differences in cost of material, labor, or overhead
- changes to production or performance standards

While the above represents the major reasons for change in Gross profit, the actual list can be much more comprehensive. What a Gross Profit Variance analysis does is to flag to company management that there is an anomaly between the actual and planned Gross Profit. It then falls to management to conduct further analysis to understand the precise reasons for the variance. Such additional analysis could be:

- purchase price variance
- labor rate variance
- fixed overhead spending variance
- labor efficiency variance
- sales volume variance
- and a lot more!

Analysts use a number of methodologies, such as 3-way analysis, 4-way analysis, and 6-way analysis to get to the bottom of differences flagged as a result of the Gross Profit variance.

Gross Profit Variance application

A business's Gross profit figure is probably one of the earliest, and most appropriate, checkpoints that financial analysts come across when preparing financial statements. Though, at the end of the day, it's the bottom line (net profit and net margins) that most entrepreneurs and shareholders care about, the Gross Profit Variance can tell a lot about how business operations are being conducted.

Growth Ratio

Figuring out how much your company can grow

In entrepreneurial terms, a company's growth rate usually refers to how the company can grow in certain areas. By calculating Growth Ratios, management and investors can estimate a company's probable growth.

Growth Ratio explained

Each year, when financial statements are prepared, analysts often predict how well or poorly the company will fare over the next period. Using that information, one can easily calculate the company's Growth Ratio.

The Growth Ratio is a measure, based on current actual and predicted future values, of how much a company will grow (in terms of metrics for specific aspects of its business), if the future predictions are met.

Growth Ratio calculated

Let's assume that ABC Company has net profit of $200,000 in 2015. The company predicts that in the next year its profit will grow to $275,000.

Clearly this is great information, but investors and company management would like to see what that means in terms of a ratio (or a percentage).

Growth Amount = Future − Current

Growth Ratio = Growth Amount / Current

A	B	C	D
Current	Future	Difference	Ratio (%)
		B - C	(C/A)* 100
$200,000.00	$275,000.00	$75,000.00	37.5

Often, this calculation can be combined as follows:

Growth Ratio = {(Future − Current) / Current} × 100

The steps involved are really simple:

1. We first subtract what the company earned this year ($200,000) from what it is expected to earn next year ($275,000). This will tell us what the incremental (or decreased) earnings (or loss) will be ($75,000).

2. We now want to compare that incremental earnings against the current year's earnings to arrive at the Growth Rate.

3. We do that by dividing the increment ($75,000) by the current year's earnings ($200,000) to get a Growth Rate of 37.5 or 37.5%.

The important thing to remember is that you need to have both current and future values in hand, and the future forecast value should be as accurate as possible. If the prediction isn't accurate, the Growth Ratio can be misinterpreted.

Growth Ratio interpreted

What this ratio means is that, if the company is actually able to earn $275,000 next year, the company will have achieved a profit Growth Rate of 37.5% over the previous year.

Growth Ratios do not have to be restricted to Profit, although that's what analysts of many publicly traded corporations use it for: analyzing earnings per share (or EPS) growth. However, let's use a slightly more complex example, this time involving a company's sales.

Year	Sales	Comments	Increase in earnings	
1	$150,000.00	Current		
2	$195,000.00	Estimate		
3	$210,000.00	Estimate		
Estimate Year 3 - Current			$60,000.00	
Divided by Current			0.4	
x by 100 to convert to %			40	%

Let's assume that company management wants to figure out what the Growth Rate will be if the company achieved sales as per the table above. We use the same formula:

$$\{(\$210{,}000 - \$150{,}000) / \$150{,}000\} \times 100 = 40\%$$

This is a great way of analyzing growth rates that need to be projected out over multiple years in the future. While statements like, "We'll sell $60,000 more in Year 3 than we did today," make sense, saying, "Sales will grow 40% by Year 3," makes an even bigger impact.

Indirect Labor to Direct Labor

Assessing labor cost efficiency

To be in business, whether you are delivering a product, service, or an expertise, you need to hire people and pay them to perform certain functions. But while you hire and pay for skills needed to actually produce/perform those goods/services, you also need to engage other types of people: those who plan, manage, organize, and support the organization's workforce.

Accountants (and finance managers) see these two types of labor in two different lights, Direct and Indirect, and use data about their costs to analyze the cost-efficiency of each type of workforce to the business.

Direct/Indirect Labor explained

Direct Labor is defined as a component of the workforce that is directly engaged in the production of the company's core goods and services. For instance, a company producing gaskets in a factory will have people working on the shop floor, operating the machines and designing the gaskets. That group of people is considered Direct Labor.

In that same company, however, there may be managers, supervisors, janitors, and IT people working as well. Since their work isn't directly related to producing gaskets, that group of people is considered Indirect Labor.

Indirect Labor to Direct Labor Ratio calculated

Assume that the gasket manufacturing company has 400 employees in total, 120 of which are Indirect Labor and 280 are Direct Labor. The ratio between Indirect and Direct Labor would be:

A	B	C	D	E
Total Staff	Indirect Labor	Indirect Labor %	Direct Labor	Direct Labor %
Formula====>		(B/A) × 100		(D/A) × 100
400	120	30.00%	280	70.00%

Using the formula defined above, we see that the workforce is split 3:7 between indirect and direct labor. For every 7 direct workers, the company hires 3 indirect workers to support the company's operations.

Now assume that the company's total payroll cost (Direct + Indirect) was $1,000,000, split into $490,000 and $510,000 for indirect and direct labor, respectively. The cost ratios would look like this:

A	B	C	D	E
Total Payroll	Indirect Labor Cost	Indirect Labor Cost %	Direct Labor Cost	Direct Labor Cost %
Formula====>		(B/A) × 100		(D/A) × 100
$1,000,000	$490,000	49.00%	$510,000	51.00%

Using the formulas above, we clearly see that, while 30% of the head count is indirect, they represent nearly 50% of the payroll cost. With 70% of the workforce involved in directly producing the company's bread and butter, they are paid only 51% of the total payroll.

Is there a problem?

So, do these ratios signify a problem? Not necessarily, since the going rates within the industry where Gasket Manufacturing Company operates may support these numbers. However, the ratios bring to light the workforce and cost distribution for company management.

If, for example, Gasket Manufacturing Company's indirect labor cost skyrocketed to 66%, far above the industry average, the above table would flag that as a potential issue. Management would then need to take appropriate action.

Direct/Indirect Labor Ratio application

Most companies strive to maintain a 1:3 ratio between indirect and direct labor, with direct workers spending nearly 70% of their time actually *doing*, and the rest 30% talking, planning, meeting, discussing, waiting for supplies, taking breaks, etc. Highly lean, optimized companies push those ratios to 1:4, and 80%:20% respectively.

The knee-jerk reaction may be to cut indirect labor and boost the number of direct workers. That is not a rational solution. By using ratios such as these and conducting workflow and time/efficiency studies, company management can better understand where labor efficiencies can be bolstered across the organization.

Inventory Ratios

Assessing how your inventory works for you

Inventory, whether it's of raw materials or finished products for sale, is what businesses uses to gauge their productivity. If you have too much of it on hand, your investment is tied up unnecessarily, leaving other areas that could use that investment starved for funds. If you have too little of it, you could end up with production stoppages or missed sales due to being out of stock.

Careful analysis of a business's inventory is important to make sure it always maintains the right balance of inventory.

Inventory ratios explained

There are a number of asset analysis ratios in a financial analyst's toolbox, and some of those relate to how inventory is analyzed. In some businesses, especially those involved in retail (such as groceries, garments, and cosmetics), inventory assets represent more than 50% of the cost of doing business. It is therefore essential that business owners learn how to analyze this main component of operations.

Inventory Turnover Ratio formulas

Inventory turnover is essentially the ratio of a business's Cost of Goods Sold to the value of its average inventory held during the analysis period. It sheds light on how much inventory-based activity goes on in a business in terms of the number of times the company manages to buy and sell (i.e., turn over) its average inventory.

Inventory Turnover calculated

$$\text{Cost of Goods Sold / Average Inventory}$$

You can get the Cost of Goods Sold from a company's income statement, while the average inventory is calculated using two values from the balance sheet:

Average Inventory calculated

$$\text{(Opening Inventory + Closing Inventory) / 2}$$

Assuming a company has $150,000 of inventory at start, and ends the period with $60,000 of inventory, and has Cost of Goods Sold $210,000, the inventory turnover would be:

$$\$210,000 / \{(\$150,000 + \$60,000) / 2\}$$

$$\$210,000/\$105,000 = 2 \text{ times}$$

This means the company has managed to turn its inventory over twice during the period.

Inventory Turnover interpretation

Like most financial ratios, the results of the Inventory Ratio are relative to each business. For instance, if other peer companies in the business above turned their inventory over 4 or 5 times during a period, then it would mean that a 2x ratio is considered bad.

In general, however, the higher the turnover ratio, the better it is for business. Why? Because it indicates that sales of the company's products is brisk, and it is able to sell more, and then quickly replenish and sell again, bringing in more sales revenue and more profit margins for the company.

Days' Inventory on Hand Ratio

If you usually sell 100 widgets a year, would it be worth your while to have a warehouse full of 10,000,000 of them sitting around? That's over 100,000 years' supply! And that's where the Days' Inventory on Hand Ratio comes in.

Almost similar to the Inventory Turnover Ratio discussed above, this ratio (often also known as Days of Inventory on Hand, or Day's Sales Inventory) measures how many days a company takes to sell the average inventory balance that it carries. It also sheds light on how many days' average inventory should be sufficient for the company's needs.

Days' Inventory on Hand Ratio calculated

Number of Days in Period / Inventory Turnover for Period

Continuing with our previous example, we see that the company turns over its inventory (on the average) 2 times a year (period). So, assuming there are 365 days in the period, the Days' Inventory on Hand would be:

$$365 / 2 = 182.5$$

Another way of calculating this ratio, often called the inventory period, is to use the following formula:

Inventory Period calculation

Average Inventory / (Cost of Goods Sold / Days in Period)

Solving this, we get the same result as earlier:

$105,000 (see previous calculation) / ($210,000/365)

= $105,000 / 575.34 = 182.50 days

This company holds inventory for an average of 182.5 days a year before a fresh batch is brought in and recycled for sale.

Inventory Ratio application

In general, companies would like to hold on to their inventory for as little time as possible. The longer one holds inventory, the less profitable a sales transaction will be (more holding cost, less space on shelves for fresh product, longer time that capital is tied up).

A high Days' Inventory on Hand Ratio could be a sign that the company's products aren't in demand, or that inventory is being held in unnecessarily high quantity, even though reduced quantities of it may be called for.

Alternately, if a company has very low Days' Inventory on Hand Ratio, it could still signify trouble. Say, for example, if the company only holds 2 days of inventory, but they take 10 days to place the order for fresh supplies, have the order shipped, unpack, and restock the shelves, that isn't good for business, either!

Off-Balance-Sheet Assets and Liabilities

The impact they have on a business

Currently, Generally Accepted Accounting Principles (GAAP) allow businesses to be involved in off-balance-sheet (or "off-book") activity. What that means is that business owners can keep certain accounting transactions off the books, even though the company may be benefiting–or hurting–from them.

If these transactions are strictly not "on the books," what impact do they have on the business?

Opening the book on "off-book"

So how it is possible for assets and liabilities to not appear on a company's balance sheet in the first place?

Let's explore two situations:

Operating leases explained

When a company buys an asset, it will usually do so by taking a loan from a financial institution. For instance, if a $500,000 excavation plant is being acquired, to be paid for over 5 years, one possible (and there may be several alternative scenarios) entry may be:

> Plant and Equipment (an Asset) Debited……….. $500,000
>
> Long-Term Debt (a Liability) Credited…………$500,000

This would bring both the asset and the liability onto the company's balance sheet.

However, if the company entered into an operating lease for the asset over the 5-year period, and then agreed to purchase that equipment at the end of that term (for its residual value), that would significantly change the way the company's balance sheet looked.

There would be no $500,000 asset shown, just a $120,000 per year entry (for example) for rental expense in the income statement.

Although the company ends up owning the asset in both cases (operating lease and debt financing), most significantly, the company would appear debt-free under the operating lease scenario. This would make the company appealing for investors and would motivate financial institutions to agree to larger loans.

Partnerships explained

Partnerships are yet another type of off-balance-sheet transaction that businesses are not liable to bring onto the books.

If a business has an interest, even a controlling one, in a partnership entity, the laws do not force it to report the assets and liabilities of that partnership entity onto their own balance sheet. This keeps such transactions invisible from company auditors and investors.

Their impact on ratios

Regardless of whether the company is technically not in breach of any laws, Off-Balance-Sheet Assets and Liabilities pose a huge challenge to financial analysts and investors, and here's why.

When calculating the Debt-to-Equity Ratio (using the formula of Total Liabilities / Shareholders' Equity) for the company above, the result will look pretty favorable, since a $500,000 liability is off the balance sheet.

Similarly, when calculating the Debt-to-Equity Ratio (Total Debt / Total Equity), the Long-Term Debt-to-Capitalization Ratio {Long-term Debt / (Long-Term Debt + Minority Interest + Equity)}, or any of the other financial leverage ratios, investors will not be factoring the impact of a partnership entity's debt or the company's own financial commitments (i.e., the $500,000 it technically owes for the equipment).

All of this makes it murky when making investment decisions.

Concept versus application

So, are Off-Balance-Sheet Assets and Liabilities legal? The answer is not cut and dry. Though the concept of such transactions makes perfect legal sense (which is why the watchdogs allow them), their application causes problems.

While it makes sense, for example, to not muddy a business's balance sheet by bringing in the assets and liabilities from a partnership entity (because that partnership is a separate legal entity unto itself), it creates a loophole for someone with nefarious intentions to mislead financial monitors.

The book cooks at Enron used partnerships to hide their liabilities from investment analysts and the public. The authorities realized too late what was going on… and the rest is history!

Operating Assets Ratio

Understanding the role of productive assets

Most companies will have assets they use during the day-to-day operations of their business. However, not all assets are directly productive in the real sense. Some assets contribute more directly to the generation of income for the business than others.

Operating Assets Ratio explained

The Operating Assets Ratio is a tool that business managers can use to ascertain what percentage of their assets are contributing to business effectiveness (i.e., profitability), and which ones are not.

Operating Assets Ratio calculated

The formula to calculate the Operating Assets Ratio is:

(Operating Assets Used to Generate Revenue / Total Assets) × 100

In general, the higher the Operating Asset Ratio is, the better a company is believed to be using its operating assets to generate revenue.

Let's assume that a company has the following items on its balance sheet.

Asset	Value	Operating Asset?
Accounts Receivable	$650,000	Y
Accounts Receivable Past Due	$75,000	
Inventory	$155,000	Y
Surplus Inventory	$45,000	
Office Equipment	$100,000	Y
Production Equipment	$1,950,000	Y
Spare Production Equipment	$150,000	
Total Assets	$3,125,000	
Total Operating Assets	$2,855,000	
Operating Asset Ratio	91.36%	
Opportunity (1 - Operating Asset Ratio)	8.64%	
Opportunity value	$270,000.00	

In the above example, the company has total assets amounting to $3,125,000, while the items highlighted with "Y" in the "Operating Asset?" column are assumed to be assets directly used to produce the company's revenue; which total to $2,855,000.

Applying the formula, we get:

$$(\$2,855,000 / \$3,125,000) \times 100 = 91.36\%$$

This means that 91.36% of the company's operating assets are productive. That would logically lead us to conclude that the business can reduce (1 minus 91.36%) 8.64% of its assets (or $270,000) to make itself more productive.

Incidentally, that figure of $270,000, which business owners might view as an opportunity for infusing efficiency, also coincides with the total of all the line entries in the partial balance sheet highlighted above that do not have "Y" against them. These include items such as accounts receivable past due, surplus inventory, and spare production equipment.

At face value, it may sound as if the solution is for company management to immediately sell off or dispose of these assets to drive the Operating Assets Ratio higher. However, as we will see in a moment, that might not always be the most appropriate (nor easy!) thing to do.

Operating Assets Ratio application

Astute business managers can use Operating Assets Ratios of their competitors or peers to fine tune their own operations. The first step, of course, would be to use the formula explained above to calculate their own Operating Assets Ratio. Having done that, the next step would be to assemble the same ratio for a list of competitors or market leaders in their own industry.

Having all of this information together will give business leaders the tools to compare how their own Operating Assets Ratio ranks against those of peers and competitors. This will allow them to make decisions like:

- Which assets could I dispose of to make my Operating Assets Ratio competitive?
- How could I deploy the cash that I receive from disposing of said assets?
- How much more competitive will such actions make my business?

Great consideration must be given in answering the first question posed above. Deciding which assets are not contributing to further operational effectiveness is often very subjective. For example, do you really need that surplus production equipment that you have in the warehouse? While one business manager may think disposing of an asset might be beneficial, another might think it worth holding on to provide spare or emergency production capacity if such flexibility is ever needed.

In taking action to make operating assets more competitive, one should also bear in mind that some assets, such as accounts receivable, that may be past due, are very much part of doing business and therefore cannot be eliminated in the long run.

Opportunity Cost

Understanding the value of missed opportunities

In business circles it is often said that opportunity never gets wasted—someone always takes advantage of it! That may be true, but even missed opportunities have a cost attached to them, and in finance and accounting terms, that cost also goes by a name. It's called opportunity cost.

Opportunity cost explained

Generally speaking, when a business owner is looking at options for investing in an opportunity (it may be a new business, an internal project, or deciding on a certain course of action), there is always more than a single option on the table. Business cases and proposals usually present such opportunities as:

- Option 1: recommended
- Option 2: favorable
- Option 3: least favorable
- Option 4: et cetera

Faced with several opportunities, the business owner must look at the risk and reward propositions of each of these options, and then commit the business to only one of these options. In doing so, the business will be foregoing any benefits that could potentially have accrued, had any of the other options been chosen.

That lost benefit of foregoing alternatives, quantified in dollar terms, is what's known as the opportunity cost. In other words, by adopting Option 1, the business gives up any potential advantages (profit, income, competitive advantage) that could have been earned from Options 2, 3, or 4.

Examples of opportunity cost

Let's assume that a business is faced with making an investment of $100,000 to diversify its production facilities, or investing $120,000 in pursuing new markets for its existing production. In the case of expansion, the company expects to earn $15,000 worth of additional sales for new products annually, whereas the marketing strategy could net the company $10,000 in new business annually.

On paper, it might seem like going for production diversification might be the good choice, providing an opportunity to earn $5,000 more annually. However, the business owner may decide to opt for the new marketing strategy instead, foregoing the opportunity for earning the additional $5,000. That $5,000 is the opportunity cost.

Why might the business decide to forego the production diversification that promises $5,000 in potential annual incremental revenue? There may be multiple reasons, including:

- complex production process for the new production line
- extended factory closure as the new product line is installed
- high training costs to train current employees on using the new equipment

It is therefore prudent for factors other than direct cost benefit to also be weighed when assessing opportunity costs. All of these aspects must be covered in a comprehensive business case that seeks to justify one potential opportunity over another.

Opportunity cost application

Opportunity cost analysis is a great decision-making tool for business owners to use when faced with multiple projects that are vying for the same resources. Business owners have scarce resources at their disposal, and those resources can only be deployed in a finite number of ways. So, when multiple opportunities come along, it is advisable to look at each of them in terms of the net benefit they will provide to the business.

Each opportunity must be weighed in terms of one another, assessing what the business will gain from adopting one opportunity, against what it could potentially lose from rejecting the other opportunities. Opportunity cost analysis makes such decision-making possible.

One key point of differential here is that opportunity costs are in stark contrast with accounting costs, which only deal with actual costs and do not consider any foregone opportunities. There are, therefore, no accounting entries to book missed opportunity costs.

Payback Period

When will I start getting value for money?

As with everything else in life, business investments usually do not bring instant gratification. Entrepreneurs know that with most projects, one cannot just sink money into a venture and start reaping benefit the next day. Every project is unique unto itself, and the period of time that each takes to deliver returns differs.

Payback period explained

It's often said, "You reap what you sow," referring to the benefits that will come to you when you invest resources like time, money, expertise, dedication, and passion into an endeavor. In layman's terms, the time between sowing and reaping the harvest is what's called the payback period.

When planning investment projects, all things being equal, financial analysts evaluate capital spending based on the timeframe required to recover the amount of capital invested in the project. Usually, that is what's referred to the break-even point or the payback period.

Payback period calculated

Payback period is calculated using two commonly used elements for investment projects:

1. the amount of capital invested
2. the amount revenue expected to be earned annually once the project is completed

The general formula for calculating payback period is therefore:

$$\text{Amount of Capital Invested} / \text{Net Income}$$

While the above two factors are important when calculating payback period, notice that we said "all things being equal" when discussing the need to plan investment projects.

Let's take a look at a few scenarios to illustrate how payback period is calculated, and how investment decisions are made using this metric.

Scenario 1

Scenario 1	Project 1	Project 2
Investment Required	$1,000,000	$800,000
Expected Completion (years)	5	5
Net Income	$250,000	$250,000
Years to Receive Payback	4	3.20

In this instance, the Payback period is 4 years for Project 1, and approximately 3 years for Project 2. Since both projects will take 5 years to complete, both will yield the same post-completion revenue. Project 2 costs less than Project 1, the earlier payback makes Project 2 a more attractive investment.

Scenario 2

Scenario 2	Project 1	Project 2
Investment Required	$1,000,000	$800,000
Expected Completion (years)	5	5
Net Income	$400,000	$250,000
Years to Receive Payback	2.5	3.20

In this instance, while Project 1 is more costly to develop, it will still be finished in the same time that it takes Project 2 to be completed. However, because Project 1 yields a higher post-completion return, the investor will receive payback in 2 ½ years, as opposed to the 3+ years required for Project 2. Project 1 therefore is the preferred way to go, even though it is more expensive.

Scenario 3

Scenario 3	Project 1	Project 2
Investment Required	$1,000,000	$800,000
Expected Completion (years)	5	7
Annual Revenue Expected	$250,000	$270,000
Years to Receive Payback	4	3.0

Scenario 3 poses an interesting choice for investors. On the face of it, Project 2 is less expensive than Project 1, and it also yields a greater return ($270,000 vs., $250,000) than Project 1. Using the formula discussed earlier, the payback period is also earlier (3 years versus the 4 for Project 1).

Using payback period judiciously

At first glance, one may be tempted to conclude that Project 2 is indeed the more attractive of the two options. As indicated earlier, we must dig deeper to see if all things are indeed equal in these two comparisons.

| Scenario 3 - Cash Flow Analysis |||
| Amount Paid Back |||
Year	Project 1	Project 2
Year 1	$0	$0
Year 2	$0	$0
Year 3	$0	$0
Year 4	$0	$0
Year 5	$0	$0
Year 6	$250,000	$0
Year 7	$250,000	$0
Year 8	$250,000	$270,000
Year 9	$250,000	$270,000
Year 10	$250,000	$270,000
Year 11	$250,000	$270,000

When we analyze the two projects a bit further, we see that because Project 2 takes 3 years longer to complete than Project 1, its cash flow is delayed by that many years, allowing Project 1 to actually pay back its investment approximately 1 year earlier than Project 2. While Project 1 breaks even (the shaded cells) in Year 9, Project 2 will break even in Year 10, making Project 1 a better investment.

In conclusion, while payback period is a great tool to use when making investment decisions, it is not the only one to rely upon when deciding the merits of a capital project.

Percent of Sales Method for Financial Forecasting

Using sales to forecast future financial statements

Businesses cannot base their plans simply on what they did in the past, nor can they rely solely upon their current performance alone. Prudent financial planning dictates marrying the two performances, past and present, to estimate what things might look like in the future.

To do so, financial analysts have a number of quantitative and qualitative tools at their disposal. The Percent of Sales Method is one such quantitative approach that can be used to forecast what a business's income statement and balance sheet might look like in the short-term future, using historical and current performance data.

Percent of Sales Method explained

The Percent of Sales Method is grounded on the understanding that most line items in the vast majority of company balance sheets and income statements usually vary with sales. Changes to these items are therefore directly related to changes in the company's sales forecasts.

Based on this premise, if a company can forecast what its sales will look like in the next year (or several years ahead), then accountants can use that information to produce pro forma financial statements for those years.

On the income statement, accounts such as cost of goods sold (COGS), taxes and dividends are directly affected by sales. Balance sheet accounts that are usually correlated to sales include cash, accounts receivable, inventory, accounts payable and, under most circumstances, fixed assets.

Percent of Sales Method calculated

In the example below, we'll use a simplified income statement for two years. In 2014, sales are reported at $1.5 million, with an expected 25% increase the following year. Using that 25% increase, we can calculate the next year's sales, COGS, taxes and dividends.

By doing the math, we are able to forecast that the income statement for 2015 will resemble this:

Income Statement ($ in Millions)			
	2014	% Increase	2015 Forecast
Sales	$1,500	25%	$1,875
Cost of Goods Sold	$850	25%	$1,063
Taxable Income	$650		$813
Taxes	$110	25%	$138
Net Income	$540		$675
Dividends	$95	25%	$119
Addition to Retained Earnings	$445		$556

Using the same 25% forecasted increase, we can build the balance sheet for the next year by inflating cash, accounts receivable, inventory, and fixed assets on the assets side, and accounts payable on the liabilities side. The increase in retained earnings ($556 million) is brought forward from the 2015 forecast in the income statement, to bring the 2015 forecast of retained earnings to $956 million ($400 million + $556 million).

The forecast balance sheet will look like this:

Balance Sheet ($ in Millions)							
Assets	2014	% increase	2015 Forecast	Liabilities and Shareholders' Equity	2014	Increase	2015 Forecast
Current Assets				Current Liabilities			
Cash	$250	25.00%	$313	Accounts Payable	$420	25.00%	$525
Accounts Receivable	$450	25.00%	$563	Notes Payable	$310		$310
Inventory	$700	25.00%	$875	Total Current Liabilities	$730		$835
Total Current Assets	$1,400	25.00%	$1,750	Long-Term Liabilities			
				Long-Term Debt	$570		$570
Fixed Assets	$600	25.00%	$750	Total Long-Term Liabilities	$570		$570
				Shareholders' Equity			
				Share Capital (Common stock)	$300		$300
				Retained Earnings	$400	$556	$956
				Total Shareholders' Equity	$700		$1,256
Total Assets	$2,000	25.00%	$2,500	Total Liab. and S/Holders Equity	$2,000		$2,661

The first thing that will strike any casual observer is the fact that, while the 2014 balance sheet is in "balance," the 2015 forecast is not!

When using the Percent of Sales Method, we do not apply the forecast sales percent increase to calculate changes to notes payable, long-term debt, and share capital. Producing pro forma financial statements using the percent-of-sales method is an iterative process, through which company management fine tunes its debt options to determine how they wish to raise funds that are required to sustain the forecast sales growth.

Company management must decide whether to raise financing through debt financing, or do so through equity financing. Each iteration of this process may be used to tweak the debt or shareholders' equity accounts, and ultimately that will result in a balanced set of books.

The Drawback of the Percent of Sales Method

Some analysts question the fundamental premise of this method: that all other accounts, except for debt and equity in the balance sheet, are impacted by sales. For instance, what if a company's production process relies heavily on fixed costs, which do not vary with sales, but remain stable regardless of the number of items produced or sold?

In this situation, forecasts for the cost of goods sold using the Percent of Sales Method will be highly suspect.

Profit Margin

What your real profit is

A business's earnings alone do not always accurately project how well the company is doing. Many analysts therefore turn to analyzing earning trends, evaluating whether the business is earning more each year than the previous year. But does having incremental earnings each year mean a business is profitable?

Not at all! There's more to profitability than simply selling (and billing) more of your products and services each year. It's how much of those sales that you are actually able to keep that matters!

Profit Margin explained

Profit Margin is one of the ratios used by analysts to measure the profitability of a business. A company that continually grows its sales revenue is not necessarily a profitable entity. Why? Because the company might well be earning those growing sales on the backs of even faster growing expenses. And unless analysts put revenue in perspective, one can't really get an accurate measure of profitability–even in the face of ever-increasing revenues.

Profit Margin calculated

Profit Margin is a ratio that helps put net income (revenue minus expenditure) into perspective. It is calculated using the following formula:

$$\text{Profit Margin} = \text{Net Income} / \text{Revenue}$$

In doing the above math, analysts are trying to ascertain how much of each dollar in sales the company is actually keeping for itself (and its shareholders), as opposed to spending on expenses to earn those sales (fees, commissions, salaries, supplies, utilities, etc.).

Let's look at the following example to understand Profit Margin:

Company A has sales of $250,000, and has a net income of $140,000, while rival Company B is able to earn only $175,000 in sales and earn a net income of $130,000. Looking at the top line (sales) and the bottom line (net income), one might judge Company A to be a more profitable business. However, that's not really the case:

	Profit Margin	
	Company A	Company B
Sales	$250,000	$175,000
Expenses	$110,000	$45,000
Net Income	$140,000	$130,000
Profit Margin	56.00%	74.29%

Using the Profit Margin Ratio to guide us, we see that the ratio for Company A ($140,000 / $250,000) is 56% while that of Company B ($130,000 / $175,000) is 74%.

Profit Margin interpreted

Simply put, Company B gets to keep a little more than 74 cents out of every dollar in sales, while Company A only retains 56 cents per dollar of sales for itself. The rest is "given away" in expenses. In those terms, then, even in the face of comparably lower sales and net income, Company B is clearly the more productive of the two companies.

Profit margin analysis application

Profit Margin Analysis is a great tool to use when comparing the profitability of multiple revenue-generating entities. The comparisons could be one company versus another or one industry versus another. It could also be used to assess which of multiple products or product lines are more profitable.

The idea is to analyze and find out how much more profitable a business venture is in terms of allowing an investor to keep much of what's generated in revenue. The more revenue a businessperson can retain, the more profitable the venture will be. Profit Margin analysis helps make that determination.

Quick Ratio

How liquid is your company?

Personal finance planners often advise their clients to build up a rainy-day fund. Why? Because life is so unpredictable, that if you have all your assets locked up in 5- or 10-year investments, you may not conveniently (and cost effectively) deal with an emergency like an illness or major home repair.

The same is true with businesses. A business owner needs to have sufficient liquid assets to deal with near and short-term liabilities effectively. The Quick Ratio is a tool to gauge that preparedness.

Quick Ratio explained

The Quick Ratio is a convenient measure of a company's ability to pay down its current/near-term liabilities using its most liquid of assets, including cash, marketable investments, securities, and accounts receivable.

Just like individuals need their rainy-day fund, so too should a company be in a position to raise sufficient liquidity, for example, by selling its marketable securities, to pay off salaries, settle supplier bills and pay off rent and taxes. If the company does not have this ability, it will:

- have to borrow money (likely at exorbitant interest rates)
- sell prized fixed assets (likely with a negative impact on its current operations)
- declare bankruptcy

None of these options are very pleasant, so business owners must always keep an eye on their Quick Ratio.

Quick Ratio calculated

Quick Ratio is calculated using the following formula:

$$\text{Quick Ratio} = (\text{Current Assets} - \text{Inventories}) / \text{Current Liabilities}$$

The Current Assets in the numerator usually includes cash, readily cashable investments (like treasury bills, CDs, or bonds) and accounts receivable.

Let's say The XYZ Widget Company has the following balance sheet:

• Cash	$90,000
• Inventory	$111,000
• Short-Term Treasury Bills	$150,000
• Accounts Receivable	$45,000
CURRENT ASSETS	$396,000
• Accounts Payable	$75,000
• Interest on Current Loans	$120,000
• Accrued Salaries & Wages	$110,000
CURRENT LIABILITIES	$305,000

The Quick Ratio for the company will be:

$$= (\$396{,}000 - \$111{,}000) / \$305{,}000$$

$$= \$285{,}000 / \$305{,}000 = \$0.93$$

So, what does this $0.93 mean? And is it good for the company or bad?

Generally, a Quick Ratio below $1.00 is a bad thing. Why? Because it indicates the company doesn't possess sufficient liquidity to pay off its current assets. In the case of the XYZ Widget Company, the Quick Ratio is telling us that, for every $1 in current liabilities that the company owes, it has only 93 cents in liquidity. And that's bad!

The company may need to sell off Inventory or other assets to make up for its lack of liquidity.

Quick Ratio interpreted

In the example above, the conclusion is that a Quick Ratio of $0.93 is bad. And that's generally true. Ideally, a Quick Ratio above 1 is always preferred. However, we should be careful when interpreting these results for the following reasons:

- Quick Ratios are usually calculated *as of* a certain date–for instance, December 31–and must therefore be looked at in that context.

What if the XYZ Widget Company knows it is about to receive a $200,000 payment from a customer on January 1? When that happens, the December 31 Quick Ratio of $0.93 will immediately change to $1.59 on January 1 ($485,000 / $305,000 = $1.59).

- The Quick Ratio is a rather conservative measure of liquidity. For example, it dismisses inventory from the mix when computing the numerator on the grounds that inventory is illiquid. Often, however, inventory may be more liquid and cashable than marketable securities.

While the above two points are valid, the Quick Ratio provides a very real assessment of a company's liquidity. When interpreting it though, business leaders must take into account the history of their ratios, as well as consider whether there are any abnormal events (such as an extraordinary, one-time depletion of cash) which are distorting their Quick Ratio calculations.

Almost every bank will assess potential lending based on this ratio. Banks consider a Quick Ratio of 3 to 1 as strong company standing.

Return on Total Assets

How effectively are your assets working for you?

While there may be a few businesses that acquire assets as a matter of prestige or status (the latest gadgets, the latest technology, the latest model; those businesses are outliers!), the vast majority of assets are gained with the express purpose of creating value for the business. And that value is profitability.

The Return on Total Assets (ROTA) is a ratio that provides business owners and analysts a measure of that profitability.

ROTA explained

It takes a number of factors within a business to drive profitability: capital, human resources, technology, vision, etc. However, investment in capital assets are almost always the most expensive/important item that drives profitability; ROTA seeks to measure how well those assets are used to generate net income (the ultimate measure of profitability).

ROTA calculated

$$\text{Net Income} / \text{Average Total Assets}$$

Some industries use a slightly modified version of net income called Earnings Before Interest and Taxes or EBIT, which is calculated:

$$\text{EBIT} = \text{Net Income} + \text{Interest} + \text{Taxes}$$

EBIT is considered a truer measure of net income because it factors out contractual obligations from the calculation of net income when analyzing ROTA.

The denominator, average total assets, is preferred over total assets because the value of assets may often fluctuate intra-year, making total assets slightly inaccurate a measure. Average total assets may be calculated as follows, using information from the balance sheet:

$$(\text{Beginning Balance of Assets} + \text{Ending Balance of Assets}) / 2$$

Further example

Let's use the following example to demonstrate how ROTA is calculated:

Balances	Company A	Company B
Beginning Balance of Assets	$200,000	$400,000
Ending Balance of Assets	$245,000	$400,000
Net Income	$88,000	$140,000
Interest	$7,500	$11,000
Taxes	$2,200	$4,700
	$9,700	$15,700
Additional Calculations		
Average Total Assets	$222,500	$400,000
EBIT	$97,700	$155,700

In the above example, at first glance it looks as though Company B is clearly outperforming Company A, with much higher investment in assets, and significantly higher net income (and EBIT).

We can use the previously supplied formulas to calculate two variants of ROTA:

ROTA	Company A	Company B
ROTA (Using EBIT)	44%	39%
ROTA (Using Net Income)	40%	35%

Using either EBIT or net income as the numerator (with average total assets as the denominator), we calculate two sets of ROTA as per the above table.

ROTA interpretation

ROTA measures the effectiveness of company managements' ability to earn net income (or EBIT, whichever variant is used) from the company's assets. Looking at this in another way, ROTA is a coefficient of the returns earned versus the investment made in assets.

In general, the higher the coefficient, the more profitable the business is. Even though Company B invests more in capital assets, Company A is showing that its management has better stewardship of the company's assets. A 44% ROTA (40% using net income) is far better than Company B's 39% (35% using net income).

A point to note about using ROTA to compare two companies is that they must be members of the same (or significantly similar) industry, otherwise the comparison is moot. For instance, comparing railways and airlines might be acceptable, but comparing railways against retailers might not be fair because of the stark differences in their capital investment profiles.

Sales Mix Analysis

Mixing it up well to make the most of your sales

In everyday life, we often use the term "getting the biggest bang for our buck" when talking about making good use of resources, for instance, when grocery shopping. The same is true for businesses when they decide on manufacturing and selling their products and services.

Sales Mix Analysis is a technique used by analysts to ascertain how much of a "bang" a business will receive from varying their mix of products/services.

Sales Mix Analysis explained

A company's sales mix is the proportion or combination of products and services that it sells. Suppose a company produces and sells three products, then its sales mix might look like this:

- 20% of sales revenue comes from Product A
- 50% from Product B
- 30% from Product C

This will then account for 100% of the company's sales revenue, which ultimately drives net profit. However, often, net profit will vary, even though sales revenue is the same (or perhaps even increasing). Why?

That's because each product that the company produces has a unique cost to produce associated with it. And each product similarly has unique sales revenue associated with it. By subtracting all variable costs related to a product from sales revenue, we get what's known as contributing margin. This can be calculated using the formula:

$$\text{Revenues} - \text{Variable Costs}$$

Revenues

In order to be profitable, most organizations will budget a contribution margin for each product/service. If that margin isn't being achieved (that is to say, there is a variance), then the sales mix (how much of Products A, B, and C should the company produce/sell) may need to be altered.

Sales Mix calculated

The sales mix for an organization should be computed by first analyzing the sales mix variance that each product is producing by using the following formula:

$$(\text{Sales in Actual Units} - \text{Sales in Budgeted Units}) \times \text{Budgeted Contributing Margin}$$

Let's compute the sales mix variance for a 2-product mix company by using the following example:

A	B	C	D	E	F
Product	Budgeted Units	Actual Units Sold	Sales Variance	Contributing Margin	Sales Mix Variance
			(D - C)		E × D
Product A	110	95	-15	$12	-$180
Product B	350	450	100	$6	$600
Aggregate Sales Mix Variance					$420

The company was expecting to earn a $12 profit margin per unit of Product A, and a $6 margin on Product B. Clearly that has not happened. That's because there is an imbalance in the number of Product A sales. If Product A is losing customers, and 95 units is all one can sell, then perhaps the company should reassess whether it should continue to produce and try to sell that product.

Sales Mix Analysis application

In slow-growth environments like we face today (low inflation, stagnation, low interest rates, low investment climate), it is very difficult for companies to function profitably, even if they increase their marketing and sales activities. However, smart entrepreneurs use Sales Mix Analysis to help them identify high-margin products and services that can be focused on driving growth, at the expense of slower-growing, low-margin ones.

Part of Sales Mix Analysis is about asking, and answering questions like:

- What if I reduced the production of Product A to X minus Y units, and increased my sale of Product B by Z units?

- What if I used an alternate production process for Product A that would give me higher margins so that selling just 95 units would still be good enough?

The idea behind using Sales Mix Analysis is simple: why spend $1 on producing, marketing, and selling a product or service that gives me $2 in profit margin, when I can use that same $1 to produce, market and sell a product or service that brings in $2.50 in profitability?

Sales per Person

How productive is your workforce?

There are many ratios that look at the efficiency of assets being used in a company, such as assets turnover, inventory turnover and accounts receivable turnover. Similarly, the financial analyst's toolbox is filled with other ratios, such as gross margin, operating margin, and return on assets, which measure a business's profitability.

What about how productive an organization's workforce is? Well, there's a formula for that too, and it's called Sales per Person.

Sales per Person explained

The Sales per Person Ratio (or Sales per Employee Ratio) gives business owners a measure of how productive (on the average) each employee is by measuring the average amount of sales generated by each member of the team.

While this is not a precise measure of each employee's ability to sell, since not every staff member on the workforce is a salesperson, it does provide employers a high-level snapshot with which to analyze overall workforce efficiency.

Sales per Person calculated

As the name of this measure suggests, Sales per Person is calculated by dividing the total sales of a company by the number of its workforce.

Formula for Sales per Person = Total Sales / Number of Employees

While the above formula is the more generic method employed by businesses to evaluate the sales generation power of its employees, some companies may want to use other variants of this formula to meet their unique needs.

For instance, a company that has two distinct business units for two separate but similar products, each employing its own staff, may want to use the formula:

Business Unit Sales Revenue / Business Unit Staff Strength

This formula provides better visibility into which of the two business units is more (or less) productive on a sales per employee basis.

Let's look at a hypothetical example based on the sales performance of XYZ Widget Company using the following data:

	XYZ Widget Company		
	Business Unit #1	Business Unit #2	Total for Company
Total Sales	$250,000	$175,000	$425,000
Number of Employees	310	170	480
Sales Per Person	$806	$1,029.41	$885.42

The Sales per Person for the company is $885.42 ($425,000 / 480), which doesn't tell us much when looked at in isolation (more on this later!). However, when we look at the ratio for each of the separate business units, it gives a sense of where the company's sales edge lies.

Clearly, even though Business Unit 2 is selling less ($175,000 versus $250,000 in dollar terms), it's 170 employees are doing a much better job of selling (with an average sale per employee of $1,029) than Business Unit 1 (only $806).

Sales per Person Ratio application

It is important never to look at Sales per Person in isolation because, as we demonstrated above, erroneous conclusions can be drawn from the results. Here are a few points to keep in mind when using this ratio:

- Use it to compare one business unit (or company) against another. For instance, in the above case, using the company-wide ratio of $885 is less useful than the individual ratios for each business unit.

- Use it to perform apples-to-apples comparisons. For instance, Wendy's Company (Sales per Person of $64,234[1]) can justly be compared against McDonalds Corporation ($63,571[2]).

- Comparing Wendy's to Microsoft ($740,484[3]) is pointless, because the business models differ, especially in terms of the people-intensive nature of the fast food industry that Wendy's serves.

- Looking at the Sales per Person Ratio for a single period can often be misleading. A company (or business unit) might have experienced short-term events (weather, labor disruptions,

---

1 "The Wendy S Sales per Employee," CSIMarket, accessed March 2022, http://csimarket.com/stocks/singleEfficiencyet.php?code=WEN.
2 "Mcdonald S Corporation Sales per Employee," CSIMarket, accessed January 2022, http://csimarket.com/stocks/singleEfficiencyet.php?code=MCD.
3 "Microsoft Sales per Employee," CSIMarket, accessed January 2022, http://csimarket.com/stocks/singleEfficiencyet.php?code=MSFT.

temporary economic downturns) that could show up in a negative Sales per Person number. Therefore, review these ratios over a long-term period to spot trends that can then be addressed accordingly.

Conclusion

When calculated and disclosed properly, the Sales per Person Ratio can provide invaluable insight to business owners and investors about the staff efficiency of a company. Higher (compared to peers/competitors) and increasing (over time) figures are a sign of a motivated sales force, which ultimately bodes well for a company's profitability.

When used for comparative purposes (such as a business unit against a business unit, or a company against a company), be sure to use entities that function/compete in the same space, or sell/manufacture products that are largely similar.

Sales to Current Assets Ratio

Leveraging current assets to generate sales

While a company's fixed assets, like a factory building or a sales show room, are used to produce longer-term benefits for the business, its current assets like cash, liquid securities, accounts receivable and prepaid expenses can be used to deliver shorter-term benefits, like improving sales.

The Sales to Current Assets Ratio (also known as the Current Asset Turnover Ratio) helps measure how effective a company is at generating sales by using its current assets.

Sales to Current Assets Ratio explained

In some industries it is common practice to hold a large amount of in-house inventory, rather than having customers or suppliers maintain inventory on the company's behalf. In such environments, the Sales to Current Assets Ratio is often used to ascertain whether that investment in inventory is paying off.

The idea behind this ratio is to analyze how many times, during an accounting cycle, current assets are turned over (or re-cycled) to generate sales. The more frequently the company turns over the current assets, the more profitable it will be. Management's ability to generate more sales from current assets is also a reflection on its (management's) effectiveness.

Sales to Current Assets Ratio calculated

The following formula is used to calculate the ratio between net sales and current assets:

Formula: Net Sales / Current Assets

Assume that financial statements for the XYZ Widget Manufacturing Company reveal the following data:

Total sales:	$120,000
Sales returns:	$2,500
Inventory:	$20,000
Accounts Receivable:	$7,000
Bank Balance:	$10,000
Cash in Hand:	$25,000
Prepaid Expenses:	$1,500
Convertible Bonds:	$2,500

Net Sales = Sales − Sales returns = $120,000 − 2,500 = $117,500
Total Current Assets = $20,000 + $7,000 + $10,000 + $25,000 + $1,500 + $2,500 = $66,000
Sales to Current Assets Ratio = $117,500 / $66,000 = 1.78

This means that the company can turn its current assets 1.78 times per accounting cycle, and convert it into sales.

It is unwise to just look at this ratio alone, and make a "good versus bad" judgement about the company's performance. If a .45 ratio is the norm in a particular industry, then a .5 ratio would be great, and a 1.78 ratio would be even better. In general, however, higher numbers are preferred.

Sales to Current Assets Ratio interpreted

The higher the Sales to Current Assets Ratio is, the better it is for the business. A ratio of 2 means that for every $1 invested in current assets, the company gets $2 of worth of sales. A ratio of .5 would therefore mean that $1 is only producing 50 cents worth of sales.

The Sales to Current Assets Ratio is most valuable when it is calculated and analyzed consistently, over multiple accounting periods. Additionally, it is best to use this tool frequently, say every quarter rather than once a year, because management can then spot trends and quickly act to either accelerate or decelerate them.

Using the ratio only over a short period can lead to misinterpretation of the situation facing a company. Perhaps the company has faced some short-term headwinds (like bad weather or relocation of its production facilities), which have resulted in a lower than usual ratio. However, over a longer term, if the company consistently yields lower or declining ratios, then there might be a systemic problem that needs to be addressed.

Analysts may also use the Sales to Current Assets Ratio with other turnover ratios, such as Working Capital Turnover, Inventory Turnover Ratio, and Accounts Receivable/Payable Turnover ratios to determine root causes for lower or declining Sales to Current Assets ratios.

Valuation of a Business

What's a business worth?

Whether you are in the market to sell your business or are actively looking to buy one, it's always helpful to know exactly what value proposition the business holds. It's all very well to say that its value is worth its weight in gold, but that's not a financial consideration, merely a nostalgic one.

Business people and financial analysts look for more concrete ways to arrive at a valuation metric. Here are a few approaches that are commonly used for business valuation.

Asset Valuation Method

One way to come up with the valuation of a business is to make an inventory of all the assets it possesses—the building, plant and equipment, fleet of vehicles, computers, infrastructure, patents, and so on—and see how much that adds up.

The business's balance sheet will be a good starting point. In some cases, the owners might attach a premium to certain assets (a proprietary cookie making machine, for example). In other cases, the asset might not be in the best of shape, and you may want to discount its book value.

Think of the Asset Valuation Method in this way: if you were to start that particular business from scratch, you'd probably need to buy all of those assets, so how much are they worth altogether?

Sales Multiple Method

Another way to value a business is based on the sales that it generates. If you are buying a whole load of assets, you want them to generate some revenue for you, so how much revenue does the business generate from those assets?

Usually, businesses are valued based on certain multiples assigned to their sales. For instance, if a business sells $100,000 worth of products/services a year, and is valued at 2x the sales, then the value of the business is $200,000. So, why 2x sales, you might ask?

The multiple is actually a function of the industry a company is in, the future growth outlook for that industry, and the competitive position the business has in its field. Today, bio-tech and IT businesses may be assigned 30x or even 50x multiples. Garment manufacturers, on the other hand, might have low single-digit multiples.

Earnings Multiple Method

As explained in the Profit Margin section, revenue does not always equal profitability. Buyers will invest only if they see the prospect of future growth in profit from the business. The Earnings Multiple Method assigns a multiple (similar to that assigned for sales) to the businesses current profit, and estimates its value based on that multiple.

For example, if a business earns $50,000 profit annually, a 2x earnings multiple will yield a value of $100,000. Once again, how the multiple is derived is a function of how well the business is perceived to do in the future. The higher the profitability expected, the higher multiple it will command.

Discounted Cash Flow Analysis

This may be, by far, the simplest and most popular business valuation method. You start off by estimating what the future cash flow from the business is likely to be over the next several years (usually 5 to 10 years). Using a Discounted Cash Flow model–Excel has a NPV (net present value) function–convert the value of those cash flows into today's dollars. That would be the value you assign to the business.

Buyer beware

While the above valuations are purely financial, there is a lot more to a business than the metrics. For instance, Tesla Motors, Inc. has a $25 billion market valuation, but it is the only auto maker, amongst the top 20 in the world, that has not had a consistent year-over-year profit, as of the writing of this book. Yet investors believe the value could soar to $120 billion over the next 5 years or so!

When you value a business, don't just look at the financials, look beyond. What are the future prospects? What's the competition like? Will the business grow? All of these non-financial factors also influence the valuation of the business.

Variable Cost to Fixed Cost

What's different, what's the same?

You don't need to be a business owner or even finance savvy to understand the concept of variable and fixed costs. If you own or rent a house, or are an owner of a vehicle, you're deep into the variable versus fixed cost game. You may not realize it, but these two aspects of expenses are very much part of our everyday lives!

Variable and fixed cost explained

Homeowners usually pay fixed costs in terms of insurance, fixed-rate mortgage payments, or maintenance fees (for condo dwellers). However, other costs, such as utility bills, gas, are telephone costs are variable. That's because they vary with usage.

In the business world, a company's variable costs fluctuate with the volume of production. For example, the amount of electricity a factory uses will vary on the number of shifts or length of time machinery is operated. Similarly, the amount of hourly wages (labor cost) will depend on the number of hours that the company's workers are made to work–perhaps even on overtime.

Regardless of how long the production facilities operate, or how many workers the company employs, costs like rent, insurance, and interest payments are not likely to dramatically fluctuate based on production hours or number of units produced. These costs are relatively stable and fixed in nature.

Variable and fixed costs calculated

Let's use another example with the XYZ Widget Company to illustrate the concept of variable and fixed cost:

For the sake of simplicity, we'll assume that the only variable costs per widget are material ($20.10/widget), labor ($110.40), and electricity ($2.52).

The company rents a factory for which it pays monthly rent of $1,500 and has an insurance policy that costs it $950 per month. These costs are fixed, regardless if the company produces 1 widget or 10,000 of them.

Variable Cost to Fixed Cost

Cost Element	Cost of this Cost Element for producing 1 Widget	May			June			
		No. Of Widgets Produced	Cost Incurred	Average Unit Cost		No. Of Widgets Produced	Cost Incurred	Average Unit Cost
A	B	C	D	E		F	G	H
		100	C × B	E/C		210	F * B	G/F
VARIABLE								
Material	$20.10		$2,010.00	$20.10			$4,221.00	$20.10
Labor	$110.40		$11,040.00	$110.40			$23,184.00	$110.40
Electricity	$2.52		$252.00	$2.52			$529.20	$2.52
Total Variable Cost			*$13,302.00*				*$27,934.20*	
FIXED								
Rent (monthly)	$1,500.00		$1,500.00	$15.00			$1,500.00	$7.14
Insurance (monthly)	$950.00		$950.00	$9.50			$950.00	$4.52
Total Fixed Cost			*$2,450.00*				*$2,450.00*	
TOTAL COST			$15,752.00	$157.52			$30,384.20	$144.69

The table above illustrates the cost calculations for the company's variable, fixed, and total costs for two months, May and June.

Variable to fixed cost relationships

Two very important observations can be immediately made on the relationship that variable and fixed costs have to the quantity of widgets produced:

1. In May, when 100 widgets were produced, the company paid $13,302 in total variable cost. That amount went up to $27,934.20 in June, with an increase in the number of widgets to 210.

2. The company's total fixed cost however remained stable at $2,450 for both months, even though production increased month over month.

This demonstrates the first relationship between variable and fixed costs.

But there is still another very intriguing relationship that emerges between these two cost elements. From analyzing the table above, we note that while the average unit cost of variable costs (material, labor, and electricity) remained the same, even though production increased monthly, the average unit cost of fixed costs (rent and insurance) declined based on increasing production.

Variable and fixed cost summarized

The above example shows that total variable costs will increase with an increase in production volume, but the variable cost per unit will remain fixed. However, the inverse is true for fixed cost, with the total fixed cost remaining fixed, regardless of production volumes, but the average fixed cost per unit declining when spread over larger number of units produced.

Cost Ratios		
	May	June
Fixed Vs Total Cost Ratio	15.55%	8.06%
Variable Vs Total Cost Ratio	84.45%	91.94%

As a percentage, the company's fixed cost represented nearly 16% of its total cost in May, with variable costs accounting for the remaining 84%. That ratio changed to 8% and 92% respectively in June, largely due to increased production.

The moral of this example is: it is often beneficial for businesses that have cyclical production to have more of their costs as variable, because then they can scale their costs based on the number of orders (or anticipated sales). One strategy that companies use to accomplish this is by outsourcing and sub-contracting various aspects of their business processes.

Vertical Analysis

An apples-to-apples comparison tool

Often, financial analysts like to present a company's results (balance sheet, income statement) in a light that makes it easier for readers to assess key trends about each line item on these statements. For instance, did the company's long-term liabilities increase this year, or have they gone down?

The challenge is: against what year are we comparing these trends to? And what is the definition of "up" or "down"–and versus what?

Vertical Analysis explained

Vertical Analysis (also called Common-Size Analysis) is a tool that financial analysts use to address the above challenges. It is used to present each of the line items in a balance sheet or income statement in terms of a percentage of a base value. Such comparisons are done for multiple years, and therefore all of the analysis boils down the information to a common comparator, hence the name Common-Size Analysis.

From a balance sheet perspective, a company's total assets and total liabilities are used as the common comparator, or base, with which to compare all other figures, such as current assets, plant and machinery, current liabilities, et cetera.

From an income statement point of view, the most common base comparator that is used is sales. All other line items, such as the cost of goods sold, operating expenses, gross profit, are then compared terms of percentage, against sales.

Vertical Analysis calculated

The general formula used to conduct Vertical Analysis is:

Percentage of Base Value = (Individual Line Value / Base Value) × 100

Let's use a hypothetical example of a balance sheet to illustrate how Vertical Analysis is used:

Partial Balance Sheet				
ASSETS	2015	%	2014	%
Cash	$42,000	1.01%	$17,000	0.54%
Cash Equivalents	$30,000	0.72%	$21,000	0.67%
Short Term Investments	$77,040	1.85%	$73,218	2.33%
Cash Cash Equivalents And Short Term Investments	**$149,040**	**3.57%**	**$111,218**	**3.54%**
		0.00%		0.00%
Accounts Receivable	$19,544	0.47%	$17,486	0.56%
Receivables	**$19,544**	**0.47%**	**$17,486**	**0.56%**
Inventory	$2,660	0.06%	$1,938	0.06%
Raw Materials	$944	0.02%	$328	0.01%

Partial Balance Sheet

ASSETS	2015	%	2014	%
Work In Process	$266	0.01%	$201	0.01%
Finished Goods	$1,450	0.03%	$1,409	0.04%
Current Deferred Assets	$1,941	0.05%	$1,632	0.05%
Current Deferred Taxes Assets	$1,941	0.05%	$1,632	0.05%
Other Current Assets	$9,202	0.22%	$7,140	0.23%
Current Assets	**$177,786**	**4.26%**	**$135,844**	**4.32%**
etc	etc	etc	etc	etc
etc	etc	etc	etc	etc
...	...	...	...	...
...	...	...	...	...
Total Assets	**$4,172,384**		**$3,142,431**	

In the example above, we have presented a *partial list* of line items from a company's balance sheet for two years. When we add the Vertical Analysis percentages to these data points, we can make important observations, such as:

- Current assets ($177,785 / $4,172,384 × 100 = 4.26%) have declined slightly over the last year, from 4.32% to 4.26% of Total Assets.

- Cash has increased significantly (almost doubling), from 0.54% of total assets last year, to over 1% this year.

- Short-term investments have declined markedly this year, from 2.33% to 1.85% of total assets.

- Despite these changes however, cash, cash equivalents, and short term investments have changed slightly (3.54% vs 3.57%) over the course of the year

Without having the benefit of placing these figures side by side, and comparing them against a common base, it might have been hard to make the types of analytical statements as we've just done.

Vertical Analysis–other uses

Vertical Analysis is a tool that's capable of doing more than just analyzing (or comparing) a company's performance from one year to another. Let's for one moment assume that the above data didn't represent the year-over-year performance of a single company; but that instead it represents the same-year performance of two separate companies.

Partial Balance Sheet				
ASSETS	Company A	%	Company B	%
Cash	$42,000	1.01%	$17,000	0.54%
Cash Equivalents	$30,000	0.72%	$21,000	0.67%
Short Term Investments	$77,040	1.85%	$73,218	2.33%
Cash Cash Equivalents And Short Term Investments	$149,040	3.57%	$111,218	3.54%
		0.00%		0.00%
Accounts Receivable	$19,544	0.47%	$17,486	0.56%
Receivables	$19,544	0.47%	$17,486	0.56%
Inventory	$2,660	0.06%	$1,938	0.06%
Raw Materials	$944	0.02%	$328	0.01%
Work In Process	$266	0.01%	$201	0.01%
Finished Goods	$1,450	0.03%	$1,409	0.04%
Current Deferred Assets	$1,941	0.05%	$1,632	0.05%
Current Deferred Taxes Assets	$1,941	0.05%	$1,632	0.05%

Partial Balance Sheet				
ASSETS	Company A	%	Company B	%
Other Current Assets	$9,202	0.22%	$7,140	0.23%
Current Assets	$177,786	4.26%	$135,844	4.32%
etc	etc	etc	etc	etc
etc	etc	etc	etc	etc
...	...	...	...	...
...	...	...	...	...
Total Assets	$4,172,384		$3,142,431	

This puts a whole different light to our analysis, as it gives us the ability to bring both companies down to common size, regardless of how large or small they each are, and compare them on equal footing. We may make observations such as:

- Company A's cash position is much better than that of Company B, perhaps making it a better investment opportunity.

- Both companies seem to be managing their accounts receivable equally well, or badly, depending on what the industry trends are.

It is only with the help of Vertical Analysis that such deep-dive evaluations of inter-company and intra-company financial data is made possible.

Volume (Denominator) Variance

Measuring production facilities

Manufacturing facilities run in accordance with tight budgets, whether those are in terms of budgeted production volume, direct labor hours or machine run time. And management is always eager to establish whether the production facility is performing as planned, or whether there are some variances between plans and actual production.

The Volume (Denominator) Variance is one tool in an analyst's toolbox that can be used to measure activity levels and assess how the facility is doing in terms of its plans.

Volume (Denominator) Variance explained

The Fixed Overhead Volume (Denominator) Variance is a measure of the effectiveness of the utilization of production facilities. It is the result of measuring activity levels on the production floor in terms of elements such as machine hours or direct labor hours.

This variance is also sometimes called Production Volume Variance, primarily due to the fact that it is a function of volumes of production, and it seeks to put a dollar value to the variance between two sets of production levels:

1. the actual level of output (units) during the period under review
2. a denominator based on the budgeted fixed overhead rate expressed in terms of units

Once these two elements are boiled down and expressed in units (volume), comparing a plant's productivity becomes easy.

Volume (Denominator) Variance calculated

Analysts use either of two sets of variables as the denominator when calculating Volume Variance:

1. Budgeted Production

The formula used to calculate Volume Variance using budgeted production as the denominator is:

$$\{(\text{Budgeted Fixed Overhead} / \text{Budgeted Production}) \times \text{Units Produced}\} - \text{Budgeted Fixed Overhead}$$

The factor between curly brackets, called braces "{ }," expresses the amount of fixed overhead which is allocated under a standard costing-based system to production.

Mathematical manipulation shows that the above formula can also be represented:

$$\text{Volume Variance} = (\text{Units Produced} - \text{Budgeted Units of Production}) \times \text{Budgeted Overhead Rate}$$

If the budgeted overhead rate is $15 per unit, and the factory had budgeted to produce 3,000 units but actual production was only 2,700 units, then the Volume Variance using budgeted production as the denominator would be:

$$(2{,}700 - 3{,}000) \times \$15 = \$\text{-}4{,}500$$

2. Factory Capacity

The formula used to calculate Volume Variance using Factory Capacity as the denominator is:

$$\{(\text{Budgeted Fixed Overhead} / \text{Factory Capacity for the review period}) \times \text{Units Produced}\} - \text{Budgeted Fixed Overhead}$$

Once again, through a bit of mathematical manipulation we get:

$$\text{Volume Variance} = (\text{Units Produced} - \text{Factory Capacity}) \times \text{Budgeted Overhead Rate}$$

If the budgeted overhead rate is $15 per unit, and the factory had a capacity to produce 2,500 units during the review period, but actual production was 2,700 units, then the Volume Variance using factory capacity as the denominator would be:

$$(2{,}700 - 2{,}500) \times \$15 = \$3{,}000$$

Therefore, these calculations have boiled down the difference between the two production levels–actual versus planned (or possible, in terms of factory capacity)–and put a dollar value to that variance.

Volume (Denominator) Variance interpreted

The results of the Volume (Denominator) Variance depend upon which denominator is used. When Budgeted Production is used as the denominator, and if actual production is less than budgeted production, then the variance shows fixed overhead costs not allocated to production because actual production was lower than budgeted levels. This is an unfavorable variance.

In terms of a favorable variance (actual production is greater than budgeted production), it represents additional fixed overhead costs being allocated to production as a result of the excess units produced.

When factory capacity is used as a denominator, and if actual production lags factory capacity, it represents an unfavorable variance because it highlights fixed overhead costs not allocated to the product. In the converse case (as in our second example), where actual production exceeds factory capacity, the variance is favorable because additional overhead costs are allocated to the product because of the excess production.

Warehouse Cost Variances

What unchecked storage costs mean

Any mid-to-large sized manufacturer will likely have a component of warehousing costs included in their overall cost structure. And controlling those costs is about ensuring that monthly costs (actual) do not exceed planned costs (budgeted). But before one ventures to analyze warehouse cost variances, one should be clear about what warehouse costs entail.

Warehouse costs explained

Generally speaking, warehouse costs can be categorized under 4 levels:

1. Handling. Costs relating to activities that put "goods in motion" from and to the warehouse.

2. Storage. Costs associated with putting the "goods at rest," meaning placing them in either long-term or short-term hiatus within the warehouse.

3. Operating. Costs relating to all activities that support the warehouse's overall operations.

4. Administrative. Costs covering non-critical, non-operational, or general administrative costs that are indirectly associated with the warehouse.

Once we understand how to classify various cost elements into these broad categories of warehouse costs, variance analysis becomes relatively easy. For instance, major handling costs will usually include labor and handling equipment (such as forklifts, cranes, and conveyors), while storage will cover rent, insurance, utilities, facility maintenance, and so forth.

Warehouse Cost Variances calculated

As with any other type of variance analysis, the formula for Warehouse Cost Variance is the same:

$$\text{Warehouse Cost Variance} = \text{Budgeted Cost} - \text{Actual Cost}$$

Usually, it helps to calculate these variances on an individual line-item basis, and then roll them up into each of the 4 categories defined earlier.

Category	Planned	Actual	Variance
HANDLING	$138,000	$148,000	-$10,000
Labor	$75,000	$87,000	-$12,000
Handling Equipment	$63,000	$61,000	$2,000
STORAGE	$80,000	$72,650	$7,350
Rent	$23,000	$23,000	$0
Insurance	$17,500	$17,500	$0
Taxes	$11,500	$12,300	-$800
Utilities	$28,000	$19,850	$8,150

In the example above, we have an unfavorable warehouse labor cost variance, leaving to an overall unfavorable variance in handling costs. Similarly, while there is an unfavorable variance in warehouse taxes, the overall storage cost variance is favorable.

Warehouse Cost Variances interpreted

The first step in addressing any unfavorable cost variance is to drill down to where the variance occurs, and then diving into a root-cause analysis of the "Why?" Where these costs appear in the income statement will also determine how their variances are analyzed and interpreted. There are two schools of thought about how to classify warehouse costs.

1. Cost of Goods Sold (COGS). Usually, when a business performs significant "manufacturing" activity on the goods inside a warehouse, such as assembly, then warehousing costs should be treated as part of the COGS, and the variance should be analyzed in light of direct costs.

2. Selling, General and Administrative Expenses (SG&A). If warehousing activity is primarily restricted to the storage of raw materials, parts, components or finished goods, then these costs are usually classified as SG&A costs, and should be reviewed when analysing variances of general and administrative expenses.

Working Capital

Liquidity when you need it

In our daily lives, even in this age of plastic money and cryptocurrency, many of us often have some form of money in our banks such as a savings account, checking account that we draw upon to pay off our mortgages, credit card bills, and use for daily expenses. The bulk of our savings may be invested in longer-term ventures like CDs, bonds, and equities, but we can't live without a small portion of liquid funds.

For businesses and other organizations, working capital provides access to those "liquid" assets.

Working capital explained

Working capital (or "WC" as it is commonly called in accounting parlance), is a measure that defines the amount of operating liquidity that a business has available to it. Though technically classified as part of the entity's operating capital, which also includes plant and equipment, machinery and other fixed assets, WC is actually a measure of the business's short-term financial health.

Businesses have both short-term and long-term obligations (debts). WC is what's left after the company uses its liquid assets to service the shorter maturing liabilities of a company. A firm that can't meet its current liabilities (those maturing within the year), will often have challenges maintaining an adequate balance of working capital.

Working capital calculated

Working capital is calculated using the following formula:

$$\text{Working Capital} = \text{Current Assets} - \text{Current Liabilities}$$

As explained earlier, liabilities due within the current year are known as current liabilities. Current assets are those assets that are held in the form of cash (including currency or daily operating bank accounts) or cash equivalents (such as readily cashable treasury bills or short-maturity / 30-day investments).

Partial Balance Sheet - The Widget Company			
CURRENT ASSETS		CURRENT LIABILITIES	
Cash	$100,000	Accounts Payable	$51,000
Accounts Receivable	$75,000	Utility Bills Due	$34,000
30-day T-Bills	$45,000	Interest on Long-Term Debt	$41,500
Inventory	$95,000		
Total Current Assets	$315,000	Total Current Liabilities	$126,500

In the above example, working capital would be calculated as follows:

$$\text{Working Capital} = \$315,000 - \$126,500 = \$188,500$$

This indicates that, after paying off its current liabilities, the company still has funds left to use as working capital for its operational activities.

Good financial management practices dictate that a company should have sufficient balance of cash or cash-equivalent assets to cover its upcoming current liabilities. Once those liabilities are provided for, the remainder of its liquid assets are available for daily operational purposes, such as salaries, purchase of raw materials, utilities, and maintenance.

Working capital application

While some businesses might tend to be overcautious and hold excessive amounts of liquid capital, others may not have sufficient WC reserves to cover their short-term liabilities and operating expenses. The trick is to strike a balance in a way that working capital isn't sitting idle, just waiting to be used, and neither is it tied up in a way that it cannot be readily used for its intended purpose.

A good barometer that analysts use to measure whether a company has sufficient short-term assets to provide for its short-term debt is the Working Capital Ratio. This ratio is calculated by dividing current assets by current liabilities, thereby indicating how many dollars of current assets are available to provide for each dollar of current liabilities.

In the case of the XYZ Widget Company, the WC Ratio ($315,000/$126,500) is 2.49, indicating that for every $1 in current liabilities, the company has $2.49 in current assets, which is a reasonably healthy indicator.

Z-Score Model

Forecasting business failures

The Z-Score Model, also known as the Altman Z-Score, is a mathematical financial model used to predict the likelihood of a company's bankruptcy.

Z-Score Model explained

Dr. Altman used a weighted system of calculations that combined up to 5 financial ratios, and corresponding probability variables, to predict whether a business would fail within the next 2 years. These computations were created to serve 3 main purposes:

1. The Original Z-Score. This score was used largely to predict the fortunes of public manufacturing companies with under $1 million in assets.

2. The Model A Z-Score. This was developed in 1983 to forecast failure probabilities for private manufacturing companies.

3. Model B Z-Score. This was used for private general companies, including the service sector.

The Z-Score is not a universal declaration of truth, in that it cannot be applied to predict every situation of an impending bankruptcy or failure. The original Z-Score was based on samples drawn from 66 companies, 50% of whom subsequently filed for Chapter 7 bankruptcy. The database of base companies has continually been updated, and the model is therefore only applicable if the target company can be analyzed against members of the database.

Z-Score Model Formulas

As noted earlier, there are 3 major derivative formulas for calculating Z-Scores, each using various financial ratios (denoted by X1, X2, X3 and X4 in the respective formulas):

1. Original Z-Score Formula (application: public manufacturing companies)

$$\text{Original Z-Score} = 1.2X1 + 1.4X2 + 3.3X3 + 0.6X4 + 0.999X5$$

2. Model A Z-Score Formula (application: private manufacturing companies)

$$\text{Model A Z-Score} = 0.717X1 + 0.847X2 + 3.107X3 + 0.420X4 + 0.998X5$$

A point to note in this version of the Z-Score is that it substitutes the book values of equity in the formula for the market value used as "X4" in the original model.

3. Model B Z-Score Formula (application: private general companies)

$$\text{Model "B" Z-Score} = 6.56X1 + 3.26X2 + 6.72X3 + 1.05X4$$

This model seeks to assess the probability of failure without the X5 variable (sales/total assets).

The financial ratios used in calculating the various Z-Scores are:

X1 = Working capital/total asset. The purpose is to assess relative position of net liquid assets against the total assets held by a company.

X2 = Retained earnings/total assets. The objective is to assess the levels of financial leverage of the business.

X3 = Earnings before interests and taxes (or EBIT)/total assets. The purpose is to measure the productivity of the company's total assets.

X4 = Market value of equity/book value of total liabilities. This seeks to measure the portion of a business's assets which can decline before its liabilities surpass its assets.

X5 = Sales/total assets. This assesses the revenue-generating capability of a business's assets.

Z-Score Model example

Let's use the principles discussed above to calculate the Model A Z-Score for a private manufacturing company called Widget Manufacturing Company using the following data:

Widget Manufacturing Company	
Z-Score Example Financial Statement Data	
Working Capital	$4,000,000
Retained Earnings	$1,500,000
Operating Income	$11,000,000
Market Value of Equity	$2,500,000
BV of Total Liabilities	$600,000
Sales	$17,000,000
Total Assets	$4,000,000

Using the data supplied above, we can calculate the various component financial ratios:

Widget Manufacturing Company	
Z-Score Example Financial Ratios	
X1 = Working Capital / Total Assets	1.00
X2 = Retained Earnings / Total Assets	0.38
X3 = Operating Income / Total Assets	2.75
X4 = Market Value of Equity / Book Value of Total Liabilities	4.17
X5 = Sales / Total Assets	4.25

Substituting the constants (0.71, 0.84, 3.107. 0.42 and 0.998) and variables (X1, X2, X3, X4 and X5) in the Model A Z-Score formula, we get the following result:

Widget Manufacturing Company			
Model "A" Z-Score Example Calculations			
0.71	x	1.00	+
0.84	x	0.38	+
3.107	x	2.75	+
0.42	x	4.17	+
0.998	x	4.25	=
Model "A" Z-Score for Widget Manufacturing Company		15.56075	

The Model A Z-Score for the Widget Manufacturing Company is 15.56.

Z-Score Model analysis

As a general rule, the lower a company scores on its Z-Score, the higher the risk that it will fail or face bankruptcy. A high(er) score therefore makes failure less likely. More specifically, the following graphic shows the interpretation of various results from each of the 3 Z-Score Models:

1. Original Z-Score for public manufacturing companies:

Z-Score	Forecast
Above 3.0	Bankruptcy is not likely
1.8 to 3.0	Bankruptcy can not be predicted-Gray area
Below 1.8	Bankruptcy is likely

2. Model A Z-Score for private manufacturing companies:

Z-Score	Forecast
Above 2.9	Bankruptcy is not likely
1.23 to 2.9	Bankruptcy can not be predicted-Gray area
Below 1.23	Bankruptcy is likely

3. Model B Z-Score for private general companies:

Z-Score	Forecast
Above 2.60	Bankruptcy is not likely
1.10 to 2.60	Bankruptcy can not be predicted-Gray area
Below 1.10	Bankruptcy is likely

SOURCE: http://strategiccfo.com/wikicfo/z-score-model/

The above interpretation is based on a 90% probability that the company will fail in 1 year, and a 70% probability that bankruptcy will follow within 2 years. With a Model A Z-Score of 15.56, the XYZ Widget Manufacturing Company is not likely to fail within the next 2 years.

Conclusion

Congratulations! You've now completed the first part of an exciting journey! As you ventured through this book–hopefully in its entirety–I introduced you to many key performance indicators (KPIs) that I hope you'll now use and leverage to enhance your business's performance. As a CEO, having your finger on the pulse of your business at all times is paramount. You can now successfully use the tools and techniques I shared with you in this book to do just that.

As I mentioned in my introductory comments, I did not have the luxury of an early warning system in the initial phase of my career as entrepreneur and CEO. But I learned! Through the content of this book, and the many examples I've shared with you, I hope I've shown that KPIs are a vital tool for monitoring the health of your business. I know they work because I've used them successfully!

Now that you have completed reading the book, make sure you don't just place it on a bookshelf and forget it. Keep it handy. Use it as a ready reference guide to confirm certain trends in your KPIs. Consult it frequently when you're looking for inspiration on how to measure certain aspects of the business that don't lend themselves to quick analysis using traditional accounting statements.

If you are a conventional CEO, like I was all those years ago before I discovered KPI magic, you'll wonder why not just stick with your CPA-produced reports? Well, here's the reason: time! As a busy CEO, KPIs are a more efficient tool than reams and reams of reports and statements.

Don't get me wrong: CPAs do very important work, and work diligently to produce that information, much of which is mandatory. In fact, most of the data you'll use to compute your KPIs and build your personalized CEO playbook will come from those statements.

The various KPIs illustrated in the book can supplement (not replace!) the accounting paperwork. For instance, when you have time, you could review your balance sheets, income statements, and cash flow statements, but nowhere would you quickly find:

- what your Sales to Current Asset Ratio is, to measure how effective your business is at generating sales by using its current assets

- the amount of operating liquidity your business has available to it, something that the Working Capital KPI can tell you

- how well your company can pay down its current/near-term liabilities using its most liquid of assets, but the Quick Ratio will tell you that

- what your Profit Margin is

- what the ratio of sales per employee is

- how quickly will you receive a payback from your investment in the firm

- whether your accounts payable or accounts receivable are positive or negative forces on your company's finances

- what the opportunity cost of making one investment decision over another is

- how to vertically (period-to-period) analyze the data your CPA has provided, so you can quickly spot period-over-period trends in changes to critical indicators, like cash, inventory, and accounts receivable

Unfortunately, the typical CPA-produced statements don't tell you any of that... at least, not up front! Sure, you could fire up your tablet or laptop, or grab the trusty ol' calculator, and do some number crunching. But if you have a well-designed CEO playbook created with the KPIs introduced here, all you need to do is look at the numbers. Instantly, you'll know exactly where you stand.

Now that you've read the book, you'll also save a lot of time. You'll immediately know where the business is headed. But most importantly, KPIs give CEOs an early indicator of what's potentially going wrong with the company, and what's going right! Your responsibility as a CEO is to:

Address the wrong quickly...
and keep doing more of what's going right!

So, what's next?

Now that you've finished reading the book, you should have a pretty good appreciation of the value and importance of this financial metrics playbook. Because they're designed as early warning matrices, the succinct nature of KPIs help distill all the noise and static from accounting statements and boils them down to single numbers for the CEO's attention.

But this isn't the end of your journey. By many accounts, especially if you intend to continue aiming for perfection in your business, your journey has just begun! In a book of this nature, I was constrained to provide you some of the most critical information about using KPIs.

There is a lot more about how you can leverage these KPIs as early warning indicators. I've learned all of it firsthand, by making mistakes–some rather costly ones–in my 40-plus years as a business leader and CEO. I believe it's now time for me to give back to the next generation of aspiring business leaders and CEOs. That's why I have produced several supplemental resources to this book.

Why just stop now, when you've just begun to understand the power of KPIs and the effectiveness they can have on the course of your business? By registering online for our upcoming eBooks, you'll be able to access a whole slew of supplemental content that'll further the knowledge you've gained in this book. I'll share with you other tips, tricks, and techniques that I learned over the course of successfully building, running, and selling businesses.

But that's not all your registration gets you. I know how valuable your time is, and how busy all CEOs are. So, I've created an amazing online KPI graphical tool, just for your benefit. They say a picture paints a thousand words. I say, graphics can replace a thousand CPA-produced accounting statements, and that's exactly how you'll feel once you've used the KPI graphical tool. The tool is available to registered users only, so get online and register to unlock even more power from your KPIs!

CEO University®
www.ceou.org

www.ingramcontent.com/pod-product-compliance
Lightning Source LLC
Chambersburg PA
CBHW052354220526
45465CB00003BA/1105